Praise for *A Stranger's Gift*

"Tom Hallman, Jr.'s narratives give a graceful voice to the universal struggles everyday people face. He isn't one of those celebrity journalists, looking at the world from afar. He writes from the news trenches and touches readers with beautifully written pieces daily. Tom Hallman, Jr., is required reading in the narrative writing courses here at Stonehill College—along with Truman Capote, Tom Wolfe, and Gay Talese. He is one of the best in the business."

—Maureen Boyle, Journalism Program director, Stonehill College

"Tom Hallman, Jr., is that rare and wonderful combination: a master storyteller and an elegant writer with a deeply perceptive heart. He has an uncanny ability to see the profound in the everyday and make you see it, too—in ways that will remind you of what's really important in life. I defy you to read his work and not be moved, enlightened, and inspired."

—Bryan Smith, writer at large, *Chicago* magazine

"Tom Hallman, Jr., is one of America's foremost feature writers, one who knows how to judge—and tell—riveting stories. Above all, he understands that the most moving and insightful tales reveal the hearts, minds, and actions of real people who face wrenching challenges and eventually find redemption."

— James Sinkinson, publisher, Infocom Group

"As an editor and a story scout for *Reader's Digest,* I've read the work of some very special writers. Tom Hallman heads the list. Through beautifully structured, easily accessible narratives, he draws readers into stories that touch the soul. This book, in which he explores individuals' journeys to faith, is moving, thought provoking, and profound."

—Brian Summers, *Reader's Digest* story scout

"On the journey of faith, we look for those storytellers who can give voice to our experiences of joy and sorrow, discovery and disappointment, questioning and hope in the presence of God, the Holy Mystery. I have read Tom Hallman's human interest stories for over a decade. We are blessed to have a great storyteller like Tom as a companion and guide on this journey."

—Rev. Dr. John Beck, Ph.D., pastor and adjunct seminary professor

"Tom Hallman's book is full of vivid stories and life experiences that challenge and inspire faith and hope in the most turbulent circumstances. Readers will learn of the inherent spiritual nature of law enforcement and the indispensable role of faith and prayer in the life of officers who have embraced the transformative power of the Spirit of God. In a vocation where it is thought that fact-based evidence truncates feelings, displaces faith, and modulates crises, we encounter the supremacy of spiritual transformation and triumph of goodness."

—Supervisory Special Agent Samuel L. Feemster (Ret.),
FBI, Behavioral Science Unit

"Chaplains have been comforting hurting people in the healthcare setting for almost seventy-five years. Faith is an integral component at the bedside as people deal with suffering and dying. At such times, people wrestle with whether God is sovereign in this journey or not. Either God is trustworthy or He is not. He is either present and caring as He promised or He is not. Tom Hallman, Jr.'s book takes readers into that world in a way that is thought provoking, intriguing, and enlightening."

—Jeffrey R. Funk, Executive Director,
Healthcare Chaplains Ministry Association

"In *A Stranger's Gift,* Tom tells how he found the right road through encounters with men and women struggling with the same doubts, confusion, and losses he was experiencing. Their stories broke his heart open. They will open you up too. Tom was one of the finest writers I ever worked with at *Reader's Digest.* Open this book and find out why."

—Gary Sledge, former Assistant Managing Editor, *Reader's Digest*

"Tom Hallman has stood in the Chicago Bulls locker room alongside Michael Jordan, hung out backstage with Van Halen, even shaken hands with two presidents, but one day a man's vulnerable, passionate story in the church service Hallman was covering for a news story stirred something within. . . . On his journey from agnostic to believer, Hallman asked the questions we're often too afraid to ask, seeking out ordinary believers from all walks of life. . . . God uses people, their tears, their struggles, their joys, and their hopes to exhibit faith to others. I can't wait to share this book with my friends. It's one I want to pass around and talk about in hopes of opening up conversations of how faith meets us when we're least expecting to find it."

—Tricia Goyer, author of *Blue Like Play Dough:*
The Shape of Motherhood in the Grip of God

A Stranger's
Gift

True Stories of Faith in Unexpected Places

Tom Hallman, Jr.

HOWARD BOOKS
A DIVISION OF SIMON & SCHUSTER, INC.

New York   Nashville   London   Toronto   Sydney   New Delhi

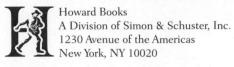

Howard Books
A Division of Simon & Schuster, Inc.
1230 Avenue of the Americas
New York, NY 10020

First Howard Books hardcover edition April 2012

HOWARD and colophon are trademarks of Simon & Schuster, Inc.

For information about special discounts for bulk purchases, please contact Simon & Schuster Special Sales at 1-866-506-1949 or business@simonandschuster.com.

The Simon & Schuster Speakers Bureau can bring authors to your live event. For more information or to book an event contact the Simon & Schuster Speakers Bureau at 1-866-248-3049 or visit our website at www.simonspeakers.com.

Designed by Davina Mock-Maniscalco

Manufactured in the United States of America

10   9   8   7   6   5   4   3   2   1

Library of Congress Cataloging-in-Publication Data

Hallman, Tom, 1955–
    A stranger's gift: true stories of faith in unexpected places /
Tom Hallman, Jr.—1st Howard Books hardcover ed.
        p.   cm.
    1. Hallman, Tom, 1955–   2. Christian biography—United States.
3. Life Change Christian Center (Portland, Or.).   I. Title.
    BR1725.H2334A3 2012
    277.3'0830922—dc23
    [B]
    2011040122

ISBN 978-1-4516-1750-4
ISBN 978-1-4516-1751-1 (ebook)

I dedicate this book to my family.
To my wife, Barbara, and my daughters, Rachael and Hanna,
who reveal daily in words and actions what love is all about.
And to our beloved family cat, Martha, a gentle soul
who lay by my side night after night as I wrote this book.
On the day I finished the manuscript she was
diagnosed with a terminal illness.

Contents

CHAPTER 1

Sunday Shift

I'd pulled a Sunday shift at *The Oregonian*, the Portland news-paper where I've worked for decades, and when I arrived in the newsroom that morning, I found my assignment—a single sheet of paper that changed my life.

An assistant city editor planning Monday's paper had left instructions for me to write about Life Change Christian Center, a predominately black church holding a Sunday service at its new building.

Fire had gutted the original building, and after eight long years of nonstop fundraising, members had bought and remodeled an abandoned grocery store to create a new home in what had been a neighborhood eyesore. My job was to attend a service, interview the pastor, and gather quotes from members for a story that readers would soon forget. That simple story launched me on a journey to discover the meaning of faith.

I'm not a theologian, can't quote Bible passages, and live in one of the nation's top three least-churched cities. During my life I hadn't given religion or faith more than a passing thought. That made me the perfect traveler for this journey. I had no agenda or itinerary, nothing to prove, and no one to convince. I let my curiosity be my guide. In the pages that follow, I'll introduce you to some of the people I met along the way. All are *struggling*—a word I've learned to take great comfort in—with faith and how it applies to their lives.

I've written two books and numerous national magazine articles, but chose a somewhat different structure for this project, as it best serves the purpose of trying to explore and explain what stirred in me that day I was sent to Life Change.

The news business has taught me that readers are bombarded and overwhelmed by facts. Answers to most questions can be found within seconds on the Internet. What we long for is meaning and connection at a deeper and more universal level.

Since I was going to explore something so nebulous as faith, I turned to people from all walks of life and asked them to share with me stories of faith.

What is it?

How did they discover it?

Why does it matter?

The familiar writing mantra—show, don't tell—doesn't apply here. How does a writer *show* something so internal? I could describe a couple holding hands and then kissing, and you'd rightly say you're witnessing love. I could write scene after scene in a church, putting you there in the midst of the sights and sounds, but as I learned on this journey, those moments are but a small part of the faith experience.

Faith is catching a glimpse of a beacon piercing the fog of life and walking toward it, never knowing if you're headed in the right direction, but pressing onward.

Faith is looking in the mirror in the morning and wondering why. It's about doubt and hope, catching a glimpse of a beacon piercing the fog of life and walking toward it, never knowing if you're headed in the right direction but pressing onward nevertheless. Even in a crowded church with people sitting so close that their arms touch, not one of them feels, contemplates, or uses faith in the same way.

My dilemma was to write about something so formless in a way that would engage your heart, soul, and mind—the three elements I came to believe are necessary to tackle the question of faith. I decided to invite you on my journey as I sought out people who could reflect on particular aspects of faith that intrigued me.

People are willing to give advice on how they dropped ten pounds in a month, improved their sex lives, or made a killing in gold. But talking honestly about faith cuts close to the bone. Some people I met told me their faith life was so personal that they'd never even talked to their spouse about how they felt. I engaged in multiple conversations with people who invited me into their lives and became what I considered my faith teachers. Through these long conversations, they showed me the mystery, grace, and power of faith in a way that made it real, relevant, and usable. I attempted to weave it together: my journey and the character's stories and conversations that—given context—became meaningful and thought provoking in ways that linger long after the page is turned.

I'm a man with hopes and dreams, with flaws and strengths, a man who has experienced good times and bad. I've butted up against doubt and ego, enjoyed great professional success, and experienced the pain of embarrassment. I'm just like you. At this moment—you reading words I've written—we're connected. That's a powerful reminder that God works through people.

A writer's job is to filter: pluck a quote, paraphrase, condense, and find certainty. I, of course, did that. But as much as possible, I wanted you with me during these conversations, listening and weighing what relates, doesn't relate, or could re-

late to your life. Narrative writers talk about a story's moment
of insight when everything makes sense. Within these pages
you won't find one moment. You will have to discover the moments that resonate within you as you set out, or continue, on
your unique journey of faith.

When the United States was attacked on September 11,
2001, I had just taken off from Chicago. The pilot was forced
to turn around and, like all the nation's nonemergency civilian
planes, we were grounded. I spent three days in an airport
hotel before I boarded a train to Portland, Oregon.

So many people were heading west that Amtrak added
extra cars. We settled in, ignoring one another in the way
strangers segregate on an office elevator. The dining car,
though, was packed, and we had to share tables. We were in a
bubble—no one knew what was happening in the rest of the
world—and we made small talk as we looked out the windows.
Then, only because we were strangers, we let down our guard.

Through conversation, we learned about each other. Not
just facts—our names, where we lived, and what we did for
work—but how we lived. Because we knew we'd never see one
another again, we felt free to ask probing, almost intrusive,
questions that none of us would have asked in any other situation.

We heard about the man battling booze, the woman worried about her children, and the salesman growing old, fearful
that he wasn't going to make his monthly figures. Instead of
talking about politics and sports or gossiping about celebrities,
we had a conversation that ended only when dinner was over
and we went our separate ways. Back in my seat, I was unable
to sleep. The conversations made me think about my life,
where I was headed and what I wanted.

Anyway, that's what's going to happen in this book.

CHAPTER 2

Tap on My Shoulder

My parents dabbled briefly in church when I was a child. They thought it would be a good experience for me and my two younger brothers. We went sporadically—go one Sunday, miss six—and each Christmas I was in the children's pageant. All I cared about was holding a fake candle, listening to the "Little Drummer Boy," and dreaming of one day being one of the wise men with the cool-looking fake beards. I never got a shot at a starring role because by the time I was in seventh grade, the church experiment had ended.

I'm sure my family, if pushed, would have said we believed in God. My parents' extended family lived far across the United States, so we had no tradition or role models to emulate when it came to religion. At the core, we were a good family—do the right thing, treat people fairly—but I can't remember a single conversation that had anything to do with Jesus Christ, God, or faith.

My first introduction to the Bible came when I was sixteen and my father gave me the Bible he'd received from his parents the Christmas he had turned sixteen. I looked at it once, then tucked it away on a bookshelf where I considered it a piece of my family's history. Aside from tradition—Christmas (trees and gifts) and Easter (candy and eggs)—religion and faith had no place, let alone relevance, in my life.

I got married in the Lutheran church my wife had attended as a girl because that's what a good young couple does. My two daughters were baptized in informal ceremonies also expected of good parents.

The closest I came to religion was at a weekly card game at my friend's childhood home. My friend's father, one of those guys who handed out tracts, could take any subject and within a couple of sentences, turn the conversation around to Jesus. We never asked questions or engaged him in a conversation about why faith mattered. We humored him—waiting for the familiar "Praise God"—and impatiently waited for him to deal.

Long after I'd moved from home, my mother started going regularly to a Presbyterian church. At her request, I attended once, on Mother's Day. When my mother-in-law's Lutheran church was looking for a new pastor, I sat in on the church's call committee selection process, strictly as a reporter looking for an interesting story.

During my career, I've been inside Hells Angels clubhouses and caught up in one of their brawls. I've stood in the Chicago Bulls locker room alongside Michael Jordan and hung out backstage with Van Halen. I've been to the White House and shaken hands with two presidents. I've watched prostitutes shoot up heroin, interviewed inmates and gangsters, and been in the back of a patrol car during a high-speed police chase through an Oakland ghetto. I even had a drink with a Mafia hit man.

I understand the codes, rules, and culture of all those worlds. Church was another matter. I squirmed when I sat in the pew that Mother's Day. I felt trapped and lied, telling my mother I had to leave early to get her lunch prepared.

The way I saw it, churches—not just hers, of course—were filled with moralistic people who thought they had all the answers. They sat obediently wearing good clothes and masks to hide what they feared revealing to the world. And did I know about masks and facades. When I was in college, I never told my closest friends about my parents' divorce.

I tell you all this so you get a clear picture of the reporter who walked into Life Change Christian Center on assignment. I was thinking about all that as I watched Pastor Mark Strong make his way down the aisle, stopping to shake hands and hug members.

When he approached and said he had a moment to talk, I followed him into the hallway, took notes, then moved on to get quotes from church members. Interviews over, I settled into my seat to gather descriptive material from the service to weave around those quotes. Once I had those details, I could return to the newsroom and be done with the story.

And then—and trust me, I know it sounds like a cliché—it happened.

This man who looked to be in his sixties walked to the front of the church and began talking

And then—and trust me, I know it sounds like a cliché—it happened.

passionately and honestly about his life. He had doubts about his job and finances. He was worried about being able to support his family. What allowed him to carry on was his faith in God's love. As he stood there so exposed and vulnerable, I felt as if he were speaking to me, even though our situations seemed so different.

Over the past few years I'd swept all the major national journalism contests, including the Pulitzer Prize for Feature Writing. I'd written a book and was even an answer to a question on an episode of *Jeopardy*. I'd reached the pinnacle of my career! I'd come a long way from when I was fired from my first job in New York City as a copy editor for a collection of home-improvement magazines.

Back then I'd used a magnifying glass to look for typos in stories about carpets, glassware, and tables. When the editor let me go, he told me he was doing me a favor because I was meant to write. I returned to Portland, where I was born and raised, and found a job at an eastern Oregon weekly paper. Bored, I moved to a Portland suburban weekly. I quit a week later when the editor told me not to write a crime story because it would reflect poorly on the wealthy community. I bartended for a bit, worked a couple of temporary jobs, and was then offered a job at a daily newspaper in eastern Washington. Two years later, I was hired by *The Oregonian* as a police reporter.

As a kid, I bounced around: five schools from first grade to high school. I worked at a car wash, a greyhound race track, as a gofer at the U.S. Veterans Hospital and a carry-out boy at a grocery store. I graduated near the bottom of my high-school class and got into college on probation. Decades later I won the Pulitzer Prize. I was invited to speak at colleges, national conferences, and seminars.

And yet . . .

When the man at Life Change finished his story and returned to his seat, I caught his eye. He reached out and gave my shoulder a strong squeeze. He didn't know me. He had no reason to reach out to me. Yet, now that I'm further along in my faith journey, I'm convinced that God works through people. That man was put there for me.

After winning the Pulitzer, all I felt was unsettled and reflective. I ended up writing a book that grew out of the award-winning newspaper series that told the story of a fourteen-year-old boy born with a severe facial deformity. I wrote about his hopes and dreams, and of the team of Boston surgeons who set out to fix that face.

While writing the book, I spent time with a neurosurgeon who invited me to watch her operate on a baby. She peeled back a portion of the forehead and reshaped the skull, pulling the flap back over the face and removing it again, fine-tuning everything to make it look just right. She even asked my opinion. I knew the baby would one day grow into a girl who would look in the mirror and like her reflection. One day, a man would fall in love with that face. I was there the day this surgeon changed the future.

But what was I doing with my life?

CHAPTER 3

Faith's Whisper

Weeks after my story on the church appeared in the newspaper, I felt compelled to return to Life Change. Something, and I wasn't sure what it was, called to me. As a storyteller, I've learned to follow my instincts.

I didn't tell my card-playing buddies, my brothers, or my parents. I told my wife and kids where I was going, but with plenty of disclaimers to let them know that I was only curious and not planning to jump into the deep end. Attending church required me to come up with a reason, something I could tell myself to make it okay. I liked the gospel choir, so driving over for the nine-thirty morning service was not much different from attending a concert.

As I settled into my seat at the church, someone touched me. Standing there was the man who'd spoken in front of the church the day I'd been there reporting. I stood, shook his hand, and introduced myself.

"Welcome," he said as he hugged me. "Welcome. How are you doing?" he asked.

"Fine," I replied.

"No," he asked, "how are you really doing?"

I stammered and sat down. I thought about bailing, but the choir started singing and the room was full. A 6-foot-4 white guy with auburn hair slipping out the door would attract too much attention. I glanced at my watch. Even if this had been a mistake, it would be over in less than ninety minutes, and no one would see me again.

At one point in the service, Pastor Mark Strong asked people to form small groups to pray. I fumbled with my program, pretending to carefully read notes about upcoming church events. A woman across the aisle walked over and asked me to join her group. There were eight of us. Jacqui introduced herself to me. The group joined hands. I felt mine sweating. I wondered what Jacqui, her hand in mine, was thinking.

She asked if I wanted to say a prayer. I told the group that I knew next to nothing about church and that I didn't know how to pray. Jacqui asked if she could pray for me. When I nodded, she asked me to tell the group about myself.

Looking back, that may have been the first step on my faith journey.

I started to get out of me. What I mean is that I didn't describe myself to these strangers as a writer or journalist. Men so quickly define ourselves by what we do for a living. But here I was a husband and father, a man who was a little nervous with no idea of what to do and worried about looking foolish.

Jacqui closed her eyes and prayed for my daughters. The words—powerful and beautiful—contained a love that brought tears to my eyes. I'd viewed prayer as something that started with *"Our Father who art in heaven"*—just words. Jacqui's prayer tumbled straight from her heart. Others joined in, offering prayers for me and my family. It was the first time in my life that someone had prayed for me. The prayers spoke to who I was at that moment and who they sensed I wanted, maybe even needed, to become.

As I returned to my seat, I felt exhilarated, as if a magician had revealed the card trick. I'd watched faith in action, up close in a way I hadn't believed existed. Within that prayer circle was an honesty and freedom, a vulnerability that I lacked in other areas of my life. I was a man of words. They were the tools of my trade. I'd spoken in front of crowds many times. Why hadn't I been able to manage a simple prayer?

As I returned to my seat, I felt exhilarated, as if a magician had revealed the card trick.

The answer was my second step of faith.

As I sat there and listened to the choir, I realized that while I found faith alluring, it also scared me. I felt exposed and out of control. Faith—if I truly embraced it—would force me to remove the mask that I so comfortably wore. Even though I didn't understand it, I *sensed*—a word that would so often guide me on this journey—that I wanted faith. I needed something in my life that was bigger than me, something more than an accumulation of awards, a title, and a résumé that I'd allowed to define me and my life's purpose.

Just the way those conversations on the train had stayed with me, the prayers lingered long into the evening. I came home and told my family what had happened. Later, when the family was watching television, I walked down to the basement to search for my father's old Bible. I hadn't opened it in decades. I turned to the first page and began reading, but found the language was difficult. Frustrated, I pushed the Bible back onto the shelf.

A few days later, I took my third step of faith.

I live close to one of the best bookstores in the United States. But there was no way I was going there to get a Bible. Someone I knew might see me. What would they think? Carrying it to the cashier would have been embarrassing. I would have lied and said I was getting it as a gift for someone.

Days later I found a religious bookstore on the other side of the city. I told a saleswoman that I wanted to read the Bible. The old one I had was too confusing. She led me to a shelf, pulled out a Bible that was written in what she described as modern, accessible language.

That night I started reading my new Bible as I would a novel. I ended up with questions. Maybe what I needed was inspiration. I returned to the store and bought a book of spiritual sayings—one for each day of the week—but quit reading after two weeks.

My intellect wanted concrete answers about faith. I was reminded of when I took guitar lessons and I'd ask my teacher to show me where to put my fingers on the neck to make chords. At the same time, my heart told me to plunge in, just feel faith the way I did when that choir sang.

One Sunday I drove a different route to Life Change and passed a hospital where I'd spent months reporting a series of stories about the hospital's neonatal unit. As I walked inside the church, I thought about a baby I'd come to know in that unit. His parents, the Van Arnams, lived in another state and were active church members. Day after day I'd watch them stand over their son and pray, read Bible passages, and sing songs of hope.

Within weeks, the baby died.

Where was God?

Now here I was, sitting in a church, a middle-aged married man with two daughters, searching for something elusive—faith—and wondering if it was possible to find it.

And even if I did, so what?

What good did faith do for little Jonah Van Arnam?

CHAPTER 4

Only Questions

I continued attending Life Change, but my fascination with faith waned. The feeling reminded me of when I'd go on a vacation to Palm Springs and spend the next few weeks back in Portland looking for time-shares to buy, then call it quits.

By chance, a nearby family friend hosted a party for her daughter who was home visiting. At the event I spoke with Jon Moore, the daughter's husband. After shaking hands, he asked me what was going on in my life. It was men's small talk: job, sports, and the weather. I wondered if I should tell Moore what I was most intrigued with and where I'd been going each Sunday.

I plunged ahead—making sure he didn't think I was what some people might describe as a "church nut." I waited for him to laugh. Instead, Moore motioned me to a quiet corner so we could talk in private.

He told me that he'd been on a spiritual journey for some time.

I had no idea. This was a man who had been active in politics and banking, and I'd never heard him speak about faith.

As a young man he went to an Episcopal church, but in time the ritual and routine got in the way, and as soon as he left for college, he quit. His senior year in college he met two girls who were vocal about faith and their relationship with Jesus. It was 1972, a turbulent time in the country and especially on college campuses. Moore, studying political science, had become convinced that the established system had to change. Politics, which he'd placed his faith in, wasn't going to solve the problems, and he asked his two friends what made them so hopeful. They told him to read the Bible, specifically the book of Mark.

A particular passage—Mark 2:23–28—stunned him because he saw that Jesus had been part of a revolution to try to bring people to what is real and true and good. In that moment—what Moore described as a split second—he realized Jesus was real.

Moore had me write down a couple of Bible passages to read.

Weeks later, when Moore returned home to Laguna Beach, California, I received an e-mail from him. I told Moore I'd read the passages, but they did nothing for me. He told me that one of his friends, Dave Everitt, was passing through Portland, and Moore thought I'd enjoy talking with Everitt, a missionary planning to return to Cambodia.

The word *missionary* conjured up memories of the pushy street preachers who hung out in Portland's public square. They yelled, held up signs, and seemed to annoy people by never having a conversation, only referring to Bible passages and saying that anyone who disagreed with them was going straight to hell. I wrote Moore to tell him I wasn't sure about Everitt. Just call him, Moore told me. On the phone, Everitt described himself, and we met in a coffee shop. After sitting down I said what troubled me when it came to faith were the questions.

"We live in a world of questions," Everitt said. "You won't find a person of faith who doesn't have questions. That's part of the design. If you don't have the capacity to question, then you don't have the freedom to embrace faith. You must have the freedom to say yes or no to faith.

"The path of faith isn't easy," Everitt continued. "When I started, I decided to look at it with an open mind. I didn't know what I was getting into, or where it would take me. I grew up with all the stereotypes about Bible thumpers and hellfire-and-brimstone preachers. I guess you could say I started with a lot of cultural prejudice."

He was one of four kids in a middle-class family. No one went to church. Everitt's father wanted him to be a businessman. In his twenties, after graduating college, Everitt moved to San Diego and got into real estate, where he discovered he had a knack for making money. By the time he was twenty-eight, he owned a brokerage, had a big bank account, and an expensive Porsche.

One day he went looking for a potential client, a man he'd been referred to. He drove to the man's house and knocked on the front door. He got no answer. He peered through a screen door and heard sounds. He pulled open the door, stepped inside, and saw men watching a televised baseball game. Everitt said he was looking for Jim. The men pointed to the kitchen. Everitt turned the corner and ran into a giant.

"My nose hit this guy in the sternum," Everitt said. "I told him who I was. He took one look at me and said he wasn't interested in me or what I was selling. He told me I'd come into his home uninvited and I needed to leave."

Everitt tried to apologize, but Jim told Everitt that his life was a "stench in God's nose."

At the word "God," I looked around the coffee shop. Would the woman at the next table assume I was "one of them"? Did I want to be "one of them," whatever that meant? To get Everitt off of God, I quickly changed the subject by asking if he'd been scared when Jim confronted him.

"Not scared," Everitt said. "But no one had ever talked to me like that. I was floored. He ushered me out the door. As I was leaving, he told me that if I wanted to talk to him again, I should meet him at six the next morning at a coffee shop."

After working out at the gym, Everitt returned home but couldn't stop thinking about the encounter earlier.

"He'd assaulted my character for no reason," said Everitt. "Every man stands in front of the mirror each morning and sees the ghosts that we don't want anyone to see. We know the stories we don't want anyone else to hear. When we stare into our faces, we know the truth."

After a restless night, Everitt drove to the coffee shop, where he found Jim.

"Dave," Jim said, "I'm so sorry I talked to you the way I did. But I have to explain. Before you showed up, I felt the Holy Spirit tell me that a stranger was coming into my life and I had to speak bluntly to him."

"What's the Holy Spirit?" Everitt asked. "That isn't part of my experience. I don't know about this God. What's this mean?"

Jim said he had no answer. Everitt would have to search for his own answer. And he did start examining his life.

"I made money and I played hard," he told me now at the coffee shop. "But I wanted a purpose. I realized I'd wanted it for a long time. I needed Jim to help me find it. I called him. He told me he worked out at the gym and invited me to join him. Afterward, we'd crack the Bible. All I knew were the words to a few Christmas carols. Jim started me reading the book of Mark because it was short and easy to understand.

> ∽✿∽
> "I made money and I played hard," he told me. . . . "But I wanted a purpose. I realized I'd wanted it for a long time."

"I was looking for answers," he said. "I asked questions. I discovered that Jim and his friends didn't just talk about faith; they lived it. There's a big difference. Faith started to develop and chisel me."

In time, Everitt sold his businesses. Years later, he and his wife became missionaries.

Evening approached, and it was time for Everitt and I to go our separate ways.

"So my questions I have are okay?" I asked. "The doubts are part of it?"

Everitt leaned forward.

"The questions we ask," he said, "are how we find faith."

Outside, it began raining. We walked to the corner. He went left. I went right.

"Remember," he called to me, "it's okay to ask why."

CHAPTER 5

Called to Explore

If I wanted to be a guitarist, I would need to listen to music; but I would also need to learn how to use scales and chords, the tools that made music came to life. Was it possible to understand faith by making that same effort to study faith's components?

I sought the advice of Annette Steele. If anyone could help me understand why listening to a stranger in church had caused such a profound feeling within me, it would be Annette.

She unexpectedly came into my life several years ago when I met someone who said he employed a black cleaning woman. The stereotype was powerful, and I remembered seeing those women during my childhood. They'd huddle in anonymous clumps in downtown Portland to take the bus to the city's wealthy neighborhoods. I wanted to meet Annette to see if there was a story about a long-gone era and the women who had remained hidden in the shadows. She invited me over.

I pulled up to her modest home one afternoon and knocked on her door. A curtain rustled, and then the front door swung open. At seventy-eight she was still spry. She hugged me, calling me "Mister Tom," even though I'd always insisted that she drop the "Mister." She led the way to the living room, where I saw a Bible the size of a telephone book.

The Bible was the starting place for her story, and it was why I needed to reconnect with her all these years later.

She'd grown up on a sharecropping farm in rural Georgia, one of sixteen children raised by her grandmother. When a man just out of the service met and later married Annette, he moved to Portland, where he got a job through an Army buddy. All her family could afford to give Annette when she left was the family Bible.

The "Good Book," as she called it, became the constant in a new city. At night she learned to read by sounding out words in the Bible, matching them with passages her grandmother had quoted daily. As a way to build her vocabulary, she'd listen to Sunday sermons and come home to search the Bible for words the preacher had mentioned. The pages of this family Bible—some torn, others stained with tears—told the story of her life.

When her husband eventually abandoned her and their children, Annette faced a choice: go back to the racist South— she and her children could live on the farm, but her kids would face a bleak future—or stay in Portland, where her children had a chance for a better life, but she had no skills to make a living.

As was her habit each night, Annette flipped through the Bible seeking guidance, and she landed on the book of Job. The way she read it, the devil had tried turning Job, an innocent man, against God by causing him to lose his possessions through a series of calamities. The heart of the story, Annette believed, was that Job clung to one truth: "In all my disappointing times, I will wait until a change comes."

Annette had faith that God would not forsake her. She decided to stay in Portland and raise the children by herself. All she could do was clean homes. She refused welfare or handouts, wanting to teach her children by example that hard work was how a person got ahead in life. When she had no bus fare, she'd walk, sometimes ten miles, to a customer's home. Her children were ashamed of her raggedy clothes. She pressed on and took pride in what her children grew into: schoolteachers, an attorney, a nurse, a business executive, and a state worker.

I knew what kept her strong during those years, but I wanted—on this evening when I sat next to her once more—to hear it again.

"Faith, Mister Tom," she said.

I explained what had happened to me in church.

"Oh, Mister Tom," she said, "you been called."

To what?

She took my hand in hers.

"To faith," she said. "Now you have to answer."

She reached over me on the sofa and pulled her family Bible off the end table and onto my lap. She asked me to flip to a random passage, the way she had decades earlier. I did so, then ran my fingers down the page until I felt it was time to stop. Annette read the passage—Ecclesiastes 8:16–17:

> *When I determined to load up on wisdom and examine everything taking place on earth, I realized that if you keep your eyes open day and night without even blinking, you'll still never figure out the meaning of what God is doing on this earth. Search as hard as you like, you're not going to get to make sense of it. No matter how smart you are, you won't get to the bottom of it.*

"You're being put to a test," she said firmly. "You been called to explore."

She closed the Bible.

"What are you going to do?"

"You're being put to a test," she said firmly. "You been called to explore."

I didn't know.

"You will," she told me.

We talked a while longer, and she invited me to join her family soon at a Sunday supper after church. She walked me to the door, and as I was about to close it behind me, she stepped onto the front porch and grabbed my hand.

"Mister Tom," she said, "do it."

I walked down those steps, got in my car, and drove toward Life Change Christian Center. I pulled into a parking space across the street and shut off the car's motor. I wanted meaning and purpose in my life. I sensed that if I was going to get them, my search had something to do with this place.

Over the years, I've studied aikido, a Japanese martial art. My sensei, a tough New Yorker, would call a student onto the mat and demonstrate. In a blur of motion the student would hit the ground. There were no words or detailed instructions. I had to watch closely to get a semblance of what he was doing. Then I'd practice with fellow students and try to figure it out. When I'd fumble or make mistakes, I'd ask my sensei to explain. I wanted certainty and answers. I wanted him to show me exactly what to do. He always refused, telling me to talk less and watch more.

That's the approach I'd take on this journey of faith.

I didn't know where my path would end.

But I certainly knew where it would start.

I thought about Jonah Van Arnam, the baby I'd watch die.

This is God's Word on the subject:
As soon as Babylon's seventy years are up and not a day before,
I'll show up and take care of you
as I promised and bring you back home.
I know what I am doing. I have it all planned out—
plans to take care of you, not abandon you,
plans to give you the future you hope for.

—Jeremiah 29:9–11

"This reminds me that we have a future.
Everyone is so into taking control of their own destiny
and life that they forget that there is someone
who has it figured out and has a plan for us."

—*Tracie Van Arnam*

CHAPTER 6

God's Absence

The security lock thumped open and I stepped into Level 3, a neonatal unit where I had been drawn to a drama played out minute by minute. As I stood above two cribs along a back wall, I wondered less about doctors, nurses, and medicine and more about God.

Two babies had been born with a congenital diaphragmatic hernia. A hole in their diaphragms let the body parts that should have been in the abdomen float into their chests. Both had been placed on a heart-lung bypass machine to let their organs rest.

One boy had no name. His mother was a crack addict. After giving birth, she abandoned her baby and never returned to the hospital.

In an adjacent crib lay Jonah Van Arnam. His parents, Tracie and Kevin, were active members of a church and visited their son daily to pray for him and the nurses and doctors.

One afternoon, a nurse pulled me aside and told me a miracle was taking place. But it was the wrong one: the crack addict's baby was getting better, while Jonah was dying.

Why had God abandoned this couple and their son?

Where was this so-called loving God?

Wouldn't this be a moment for God to reveal Himself?

I waited around the unit one afternoon to watch Kevin and Tracie get the bad news. A doctor compassionately told them the truth and asked what they wanted for Jonah.

"Jonah has a closer connection to God at this moment than I do," his mother said. "Jonah's looking at both sides and figuring out which is better. Heaven or Mom and Dad. I told him if his soul is hanging on because of me, because I want him, to let go, go be with God."

During the report the next evening, the supervisor told the night-shift nurses that Jonah's parents had made their decision.

"We have some friends, relatives, out there in the hall," Kevin told a nurse. "We're going to bring them in to say goodbye."

Monitors no longer needed to be checked. The only medicine flowing into Jonah's body was morphine to make his last moments painless. One by one, friends and family said farewell to the child. Then the parents were alone.

Minutes later, a doctor arrived and explained to the Van Arnams how the lines would be removed from Jonah. When they were ready to let their son go, they'd tell a nurse, who would disconnect the ventilator. Two nurses began taking away nonessential lines while others cleaned Jonah, wrapped him in a blanket, and placed the boy in his mother's arms. She had never held her son.

"I'm so sorry," Tracie told Jonah. "I'm so sorry."

The life-support monitor had gone black and silent. The only remaining sound was the thump-thump-thump of the ventilator.

"We're ready," Tracie said.

A nurse pulled the ventilator tube from Jonah's mouth and flipped off the ventilator; the thumping stopped. Late that night, the Van Arnams left Level 3. Their son's body remained behind. A family member made arrangements for a funeral at the couple's church.

Now, as I stumbled along on my faith journey, I thought back to that night in 2003 and wondered what Tracie could teach me. I searched through my old notes and found her telephone number. The phone rang three times. I recognized her voice. I explained why I was calling. There was a long pause, as if she was thinking about what I had asked.

I heard a tremble in her voice.

"Everything I had ever heard a preacher say, everything I had ever heard in church, everything I'd ever read in the Bible rushed at me from the day I learned Jonah was sick until the day he died," she said. "Everything I wanted or hoped for was called into question. If you want to know about my faith, then we'll have to start at the beginning."

I drove with one hand, looked at the address scratched on a piece of paper resting on my lap, eased off the gas pedal, parked, and walked to the front door.

Tracie opened it. Their daughter, Emma, emerged from behind her. In the living room I saw Kevin holding the baby, born years after Jonah's death. The family ushered me inside. I felt as if I were meeting the parents on a blind date. I made small talk about the big-screen television, picture quality, and how work was going. Finally, there was nothing left to talk about other than why I had driven more than three hours to see them.

"I prayed for perfection, a healthy baby," Tracie said. "The Bible says come expecting, for what you want. I did. Everyone did the best they could. All the doctors and all the nurses. Sometimes we don't always get the outcome we want."

I asked the question that had haunted me for so long:

Why didn't God make Jonah better? I told Tracie about what it had been like for me, learning the circumstances of the baby next to Jonah.

"No," Tracie said. "No."

She began crying.

"I never knew about that other baby's background," she said. "A crack-addict mother?"

I feared I'd divulged information that had ripped open a scab. Perhaps it best I leave. Tracie shook her head. To gather herself, she walked to the kitchen to make us sandwiches. She returned, set the platter in the middle of the table, and asked why I was so interested in God and Jonah. I brought her up to date on what had happened to me.

"Seems like you're making faith awful weighty," she said. "Sometimes there's just a relief in submitting to faith."

Perfect sense, I said, when you're talking about faith when times are good. I leaned across the table.

"You had a baby die," I said. "How could you ever believe again?"

She took Kevin's hand in hers.

"That night Kevin and I prayed," she said. "We were looking for guidance and peace. How did we know if we were doing the right thing? I wondered if the prayer was effective. I wondered if God heard us. Then I knew what we had to do. We had to let our son go."

I told her that she made it sound so simplistic, and that was one of the things that made me question Christians who professed such strong faith. No matter the circumstance, it seemed they always had a pat answer—"God's plan"—that let God off the hook. These same Christians who could get so mad at their spouse for a small infraction—not cleaning the kitchen or taking out the garbage—refused to hold God accountable.

I couldn't accept that Jonah's fate had been that easy to accept.

Never easy, Tracie said quietly, explaining that the real hell wasn't in the hospital but in the real world—in fact, in the church, the place I'd assumed would be a source of comfort and understanding.

"My anger started a week after Jonah's death," she said. "We buried him on Friday and went to church that Sunday. Someone there told me that God must have needed Jonah in heaven. I walked away. But I was so mad that I turned around and came back to this person. I said that God does not need my son, so shut up."

Her honesty surprised me.

"My anger was all at God, but it landed on people," she said. "I wasn't leaning on God. I was furious. I'd run the race so well and finished it. But I didn't get the prize—a healthy baby to take home with us.

"I was raw and honest," she said. "People we thought were our best friends went out of their way to say they couldn't be in our lives anymore because we were not in the same season they were. I asked what season were they talking about, and they said we'd lost a child. I see now that I was putting my faith in people, not God."

I asked her how she could learn to trust God again. Jonah's death, to me, proved God had betrayed the family.

"I didn't pray like I used to," she admitted. "I didn't connect with faith the way I once had. I was never disconnected from God, but I know what it feels like to want to be disconnected. You are grieving and hurting, and the pain is so great, you want to get in bed, pull the covers over your eyes, and go to sleep. But I kept hearing God's voice telling me it was okay to be mad at Him. He had big shoulders."

I told Tracie that made her seem quite religious.

"I'm not religious and don't like being called religious," she said. "What I have is a friendship and kinship with the Lord. All He wants from me is my heart."

Time passed and we talked about God, faith, and pain.

"Tracie," I asked, "why was Jonah born?"

She sighed.

"I think about that all the time," she said. "You know I kept in touch with the nurse who was with me the night Jonah died. She later told me that she had miscarried and after seeing what people went through in that neonatal unit, she wasn't sure she wanted a baby. I told her that living in fear robs you of life. She ended up having a baby. That conversation I had with her—that little blip—could have been the only reason that Jonah died."

She smiled a sad smile.

"Why did Jonah have to go?" she asked. "I never heard an answer."

At that crossroads, I asked, why choose faith?

The Van Arnams appeared to have signed a so-called faith contract: church, prayer, reading the Bible, and living a life committed to the love and teaching of Jesus Christ. The Savior who performed miracles in the Bible couldn't find it possible to let Jonah live? That crack-addict baby, the last I had heard, had been turned over to the state.

"I am in the world, but not of the world," she said. "As a mature Christian, I realize that means I'm not meant to know everything. I'm a pretty driven person. I wouldn't consider myself weak, but it took me a couple of years to work through this. I still have moments when it feels like it was yesterday.

"People in the church didn't know what to do with me," she said. "Just because people are in a church doesn't make them better, me included. I was just trying to get through the same struggles as everyone else. We left that church and later found another one. We needed change. We were broken people. It was horrid. You have to be wise in your walk with the Lord. He doesn't just fix things. You have to do the work. Faith was part of it. I couldn't move forward until I dealt with the hurt and anger I felt toward God."

"You have to be wise in your walk with the Lord. He doesn't just fix things."

She wiped her eyes once more.

"People who don't understand faith, don't think you can be mad at God," she said. "They think that's wrong. But you can. It's a relationship with God. There are challenges, some of them terrible, that He wants us to get through. He helps through faith, and by working through humans to accomplish that.

"Our dear friends were with us when Jonah died. Jonah was born on July seventh and their son on September fifth," she said. "They went through such guilt. I never felt bitter toward them, but when I see their son, I remember what it would be like to have Jonah. We would have three kids. Sometimes my heart aches."

What, I asked Tracie, did you want from God?

"Another part of faith is restoration and healing," she said. "At the heart of the matter, I wanted to be whole and healed. Faith did that for me. We were able to help other parents going through the death of a child, the worst moment that can happen to a parent."

I told her it must have been a horrible night. She said nothing, just stared at me as if weighing what she wanted to say.

"What I remember about that night is you sitting there, Tom," she said. "I so badly wanted to turn to you and say 'Did you get all that?' We let you be there, but I was so mad at you at the end of the night because you got to go home.

"To you, it was just a story," she said. "You didn't have to live behind the curtain and turn off the button that kept your son alive. A part of me wanted you to get off your butt, turn that recorder off, and see what it was like to have made that decision."

By now she knew more about me and what I was seeking.

"Your job puts you in a unique position," she said, her tone softening. "You see all these things and talk to all these people. It passes through you. You're dealing with the oldest questions on the planet. Is there a God? Is He really after my best interests? Where do I fit in with faith?

"You've been asked to do something—get stories," she said. "You'll never get the one answer. But the journey will be good. I can tell you that the faith journey is made up of all kinds of things. Some are extreme, like us losing a baby. Some are quiet, the daily things that you, and only you, see.

"As in life," she said, "there is no map for the faith journey."

The cemetery was right off the freeway. I turned into the parking lot and spoke to a man behind the front desk. He handed me a map, showed me the path to take, outlining it with a red pen. I stood in the front doorway. In the distance I saw the U-shape hedge that holds the graves of the children. He was in the second row. The gravestone was no bigger than a laptop computer: *Jonah Jonn Van Arnam*. He lived nearly twenty days.

I stared at that piece of granite, remembering his last night in the hospital and all his mother had told me during our recent conversation. To her it made sense. But for me—a faith skeptic—I had only unresolved questions.

If the point of prayer was to communicate with God, why wouldn't He answer a plea from devoted parents? The Van

Arnam family had done everything right by God. I couldn't accept that a baby who had never spent a moment outside of a neonatal unit was a sinner.

Had they failed God? If so, what more could a loving God want from them?

Had God failed them? If so, what was the point of believing in an all-powerful force that remained on the sidelines while doctors desperately tried to save a baby's life?

I clearly lacked theologically sound answers. Perhaps that was my stumbling block. I wanted to find someone whom I was sure had no doubts and could convince me that not only was God real but also that faith mattered. But at this moment—standing in a cemetery as a parent—it felt so wrong.

At the end of the row I found a wooden bench and sat down.

Tracie Van Arnam had told me that God knows what is in our hearts. Then He certainly knew the questions I was grappling with. I waited for a sign that revealed to me that God cared about that little boy, and that in the coming years He would provide comfort and love to Jonah's parents.

In the silence I listened for a voice inside of me, a call from the spirit—anything to offer me an indication that it had not been all for naught.

I felt nothing.

So I just sat there, feeling the sun on my neck, listening to the birds, and watching the wind play with the trees.

*Through thick and thin, keep your hearts at
attention, in adoration before Christ, your Master.
Be ready to speak up and tell anyone who asks why
you're living the way you are,
and always with the utmost courtesy.*

—1 Peter 3:15

"There is a reason for hope."

—*Pastor Red Burchfield*

CHAPTER 7

Doubting Thomas

Sunday services had ended hours earlier and Brian Burch-field was alone in his church. It had been a long day—the sermon, the coffee hour, planning hospital visits, and figuring out the church budget. He was weary as he walked through the hallways, turning off lights and locking doors as he made his way to his office. With a sigh he settled into a leather chair behind his desk. He had but a moment to relax because he knew the phone would ring. A good friend had recently died. He expected the man's wife would call, hoping he could provide a few comforting words.

He undid his shirt collar, pulling out the white plastic that told the world he was a pastor. He set it on his desk, studying the tab in the same way a bird of prey examines something from high in the sky. So small—no larger than a King Size Snickers bar—and yet so powerful. He leaned forward, picked up the tab, twisting it this way, almost as if he were seeing it for the first time.

This boy will be a pastor.

Even now he could hear that proclamation, the words that made his father so proud and him so angry.

When a man reflects on his life, it's often hard to see all the forces that guided and shaped him. Not for Pastor Burchfield. His script was written the day he was baptized. The pastor at his family's church performed the ceremony and told all who had gathered that little Brian Burchfield would grow up to be a pastor.

This was no ordinary, see-you-on-Sunday pastor. He was considered part of the Burchfield family. Brian's parents—two schoolteachers who met and married in South Dakota—had moved to Alaska, where Brian's father was stationed during WWII. They'd joined a church, and the older pastor and his wife had taken the young couple under their wing. When Brian was born, the pastor considered the boy to be his grandson, and Brian called him Grandpa for the rest of his life.

This boy will be a pastor.

Sitting in his office this Sunday, Pastor Brian Burchfield—known informally as Pastor Red because of the color of his hair—thought about how many times his father told that story, with such pride and certainty, to friends, relatives, and even strangers.

A father sees his kid smack several home runs in Little League, and it's natural that he starts bragging about having a future all-star in the family, the kid who will one day roam center field for the New York Yankees. Then reality sets in, and by high school the father's dreams have faded.

But this pastor's prophecy was like a word straight from God. And who questions God?

As he grew, Brian hated the story. His father would start in, setting the scene at the baptism and the great man's words, and Brian felt as if the walls were closing in on him and his destiny. His life was being charted out for him without any input about what he wanted or dreamed of. In the fourth grade, Brian's teacher told the students their assignment was to write a report about what they wanted to be when they grew up. Brian panicked. What ten-year-old boy stands in front his peers and says he's going to be a pastor? He lied, coming up with something that wouldn't make people laugh at him. But the words had been so seared into his soul, become such a part of his DNA and destiny that he could not run from the truth or alter the course of his future.

After college, of course, Burchfield enrolled in seminary. Two years in and after an internship, he took a leave of absence. He was haunted by a simple question he'd never had the courage to ask: Did he have to be a pastor?

By then he wondered if it was too late to choose. He was married and had two daughters. He escaped seminary, taking his family across the country to New York City, where he ran a group home for kids. For the first time in his life, he felt as if he were writing his own story. He discovered a meaningful profession where he could help in ways that had nothing to do with being a pastor.

Freed from the shackles, he confronted his father, laying it all out in anger how that six-word sentence, repeated so insistently, had set the course of his life for as long as he could remember. Why had it been so important to his father? Why had that pastor held such power?

Once the anger was out, though, Burchfield knew with all his heart that he *did* want to be a pastor. He returned to seminary and completed the program. That was the moment he felt he first understood the deep mystery of faith.

He claimed his own life story by living out his understanding of what it means to follow Jesus Christ. Anyone can do that: a cabdriver or a commercial fisherman. But since he had the interest, passion, and imagination for engaging people in what he called "conversations about the journey of faith," it made sense he was a pastor.

The telephone rang in Pastor Red's office.
His wife's friend was on the line.

Tracie Van Arnam's pointed question to me—was I going to
get off my butt and explore faith?—made me recalibrate where
I needed to go. I wasn't capable of blind faith because I had too
many questions: Is faith something all humans have deep inside of us? Is faith brought to life because of a series of events?
Or is faith simply a story taught to kids in Sunday School, a
story they never question as they grow older?

Even the notion of faith felt quaint. With all this technol-
ogy in our world, why was faith even important?

How did it enrich my life, and what was in it for me?

At some level I sensed that faith didn't have a specific link
to the Bible, the church, or even the pastor. I couldn't articulate it, but I knew that if I wanted to embrace faith, I had to
have the courage to let go and be vulnerable. Once again, I
saw it as an internal battle.

I needed a reason, an excuse really, to incorporate faith in
my life in a way that made intellectual sense to me. I wanted
experts to tell me it was okay. Who better than a pastor? I
didn't know Life Change's Pastor Mark Strong well enough to
talk with him. I felt I'd be disrespectful, coming across as an
investigative reporter with an ax to grind. I knew of no one in a
position of theological authority where I could be intellectually
honest—asking what could seem to be stupid questions and
pressing this person to sell me on faith and why it mattered
not to the world, but to me.

And then I thought of Pastor Red.

I'd first met him when I was writing a story about the call
committee at Portland's Central Lutheran Church. I sat in on
the interviews and liked the way Pastor Red handled himself

by answering a series of wide-ranging questions. He had long ago moved from Central Lutheran, but I tracked him down at a Seattle, Washington, church and called, telling him a bit of what I'd been going through. I told him I needed to talk about issues in my life and that I didn't know where else to turn.

When I arrived, he led the way to his office, where I filled him in on my quest: the newspaper story assignment, my church attendance, and my faith stirrings that were both joyful and perplexing.

He leaned back in his chair, listened, and then smiled.

"You've been given a gift," he said.

I said I was confused.

"People—and I would be so bold as to say all people—have the same questions you have," he said. "What they don't have is the necessary courage you have to let them come to the surface. They have the same stuff rolling around inside their heads and hearts, but they have not cultivated the readiness to entertain the challenge those questions bring to a life."

My questions, Pastor Red explained, were an invitation, to explore faith on a more thoughtful and deeper level.

As much as I appreciated the compliment, I looked to him to give me answers. I wasn't looking for a philosophical discussion. I wanted him to reach behind his desk, rummage through the bookshelf, and toss me an owner's manual for faith. Clearly it doesn't exist, but if I take my car to a mechanic, he can explain how a transmission works, show me diagrams, and even put the car on the lift to

> I wasn't looking for a philosophical discussion. I wanted him to reach behind his desk, rummage through the bookshelf, and toss me an owner's manual for faith.

let me see the gears. Maybe I was naive, but I assumed that a pastor could answer the questions that so troubled me.

"I wish is it were so simple," he said. "I have no answers for you."

He slapped his hands on the table.

"None," he said. "Faith is a journey, and we don't have a guidebook or a map to help us on this trip. At its best the Bible—to use psalm 119, verse 105, *'Your word is a lamp to my feet and a light to my path'*—is God's word to us. The psalms are the prayer book of the Bible. They give voice to many of our thoughts and emotions in our journey of faith. Some of these questions are the same things you are grappling with."

I wrote myself a note: Read Bible each night. Pastor Red noticed and held up his hand as a warning.

"What we don't want to do is to reduce—perhaps out of our own human anxiety—the story of God's love to a rule book," he said. "God's love is a story, and through that story love is transmitted to us."

At least now we were speaking my language. I understood story, and Pastor Red asked me what I thought he meant. I told him that a story unlocks what's in us already and makes us feel connected. During my career, I'd found stories that used a character's situation—even though it was so unlike the reader's—to explore something much deeper, something that reminded us of our shared humanity.

Pastor Red nodded.

"Story helps us discover what is truer than facts," Pastor Red said. "Doesn't that sound like faith? There are no facts when it comes to faith. But there is something truer than facts. You sense faith. You feel faith.

"The Bible and the metaphors embody and express the deepest truth of the universe," he continued. "A story provides multiple levels of access. You hear the story and it engages you at your edge of readiness to faith. Someone else reads the same story and it engages them where they are on their faith journey. If it is really a well-crafted story, it is also in harmony with the deepest rhythms of the universe."

I understood that—kind of—but asked him who was supposed to help me make sense of the story if it wasn't people like him, men and women who had gone to seminary, knew theology, and made a career out of study, preaching, and guiding church members who came each Sunday seeking words of wisdom. Now he was telling me there was no imaginary faith finish line that I could cross and say I knew enough to no longer struggle with faith.

"What was it you said intrigued you about faith as it relates to you?" he asked. "Not faith in terms of the Bible and of church and of prayer, but faith and you, just one man making his way in the world?"

I answered easily: letting go of myself. But the struggle was difficult. I didn't want to let go. Or maybe, on a good day, just a little bit. And if I did let go of myself, I wanted to get something out of it. Until then, I wanted to hold out my options.

"There you are," he said. "That's this hard conversation. If we are thoughtful people of faith, we sometimes have to say what something is not. We have to tell the truth. And to whom? Ourselves. When we equate faith with simply understanding faith, we have made faith something that we own, manage, control, and possess.

"It is no longer faith," he said. "It is now in our jurisdiction. Reducing Christian faith to a set of rules, principles, and understandings leads us away from biblical faith and the living God behind that conversation that is so necessary. We trust there is something more to the universe than just us. Faith means that we say we will never fully know, except as the Holy Other chooses to be revealed.

"Think about the idea that there is something greater than you and me," Pastor Red said. "Not just the prime mover and first cause, although that can be a part of it, but something that seeks and longs to be in relationship with us. That is the heart of the biblical story. That is the covenant.

"If we are willing to engage in the conversation about the Other," he said, "then we have to be willing to acknowledge that our understanding of that relationship is not an exhaustive understanding and may not be an accurate description."

I hadn't driven three hours to Seattle and spent the night in a hotel room for this. It sounded like a lot of faith doubletalk. So you're telling me, I asked, that there's a lot I'll never understand when it comes to faith?

He nodded.

Why, I asked—and apologized for the word I was going to use—is faith so damn hard?

It's a breeze on a Sunday morning in church. But the moment I walk outside, I'm hit with life's complexities, and faith seems to have as much power in that complex world as a rabbit's foot or four-leaf clover.

"Faith is trust," Pastor Red said. "When we experience challenges in our life, we see more clearly what we are trusting in and what our assumptions and presumptions are. Life is filled with grief. Life is never what you and I would expect or hope it would be.

So why, I asked, do we need pastors?

"There's an old story about a Sufi, a master, who takes a group into the wilderness," Pastor Red explained. "They lose their way, and they wander and wander and come upon another group. The second group says they've lost their way and they ask for help. The Sufi said he can't lead them out of where they are, but he may be able to help. His group, too, has lost its way. And he knows a hundred trails that are not the right way out. That's what pastors are.

"The holy man or woman is not holy for something they do," he said. "God sets them apart for a purpose, to live lives that reflect God's love to the world and share in the journey. The holy man or woman is the person who is willing to be lonely on behalf of the community. The person who is willing to struggle with the questions that the community doesn't quite know how to ask or might not have the courage, at this time in their life, to wrestle with."

So you grapple with the questions? You struggle with your faith?

"All the time," he admitted. "God calls us to be in a relationship, one that is living and dynamic. It is a relationship that has highs and lows; at times it is strong and then weaker. We are writing our story as we live it. What we do is take the overriding story—relationship with God—and make it our own. There is the mega-narrative—being drawn into God's love. Within that story there is an enormous range of freedom in this partnership that God calls us into. And then there are the overriding stories, the influences on your life and my life. All of those are at work on us as we are called to sort out the overriding story."

Does it matter if I don't get an answer? Is the pursuit of the question enough?

"We should talk about faith as a gift that God gives us," he said. "The New Testament would say that even the ability to say 'I believe' can only happen as you receive it as a gift from God. Left to our own devices, we curve back onto ourselves. And if this is where we go, we cannot look to ourselves to transform ourselves. We're not going to get a quick fix. For us to change, something has to break in from the outside."

That makes it sound as if faith is almost like therapy. We end up in a counselor's office because we can't fix ourselves.

"That is exactly right," he said. "The God of the Bible is made known in Jesus. God, in a sense, seduces us. God created the world in goodness, and that includes all of us. But it fell apart. The reality of this condition is that something must break in from the outside to change who we are as people. Faith is the gift God puts within us. It is the capacity to trust that we are not alone. A knowledge that we are loved. A belief that we are loved, that we are of infinite value, and that this life is not all there is."

If I say I am a man of faith, why does that have such a bad connotation with so many people who make assumptions about faith and what it means? What if someone who has no faith and claims to never want it tells you that faith is a bunch of self-help nonsense?

"My response: God bless you, brother," he said. "I don't need to fix him. If we say that faith is a gift, then that is not my job. My job is to witness to this Elusive One. When I reduce faith to a set of certainties, I tend to be bragging. I do things right and thumb my nose at you. Sometimes people of faith are poor reflections of the inclusive love of God. I think the mysterious and elusive creator of the universe grabs hold of us by faith; faith is about being drawn into that passionate relationship in which we are invited to trust."

It seemed okay—perhaps expected—that I would struggle with faith. But what about Pastor Red?

"Even when I seem full of faith, I ask for help with my unbelief," he said quietly. "Maybe the only difference between me and you is that I have tried to explore the hundreds of roads that are not the right way."

I had sought an expert. What I saw across the desk was a man just like me. I found it comforting that he didn't have all the answers.

"That would be the setup to believe that I am an author-ity," he said. "I have no definite answer. I can tell you what's in-teresting. I can tell you little things. Mostly that faith is a relationship of trust. An analogy is the marriage relationship. Am I going to trust my wife will love me, hell or high water? Will she be there when I am at my worst? Do I trust that she will not abandon me, even when I try to abandon her? Faith with God is like that. There's a knowing, a vulnerability that transcends our capacity to even name it clearly."

Will I ever get my answer? Or will I get one answer fol-lowed by yet another question? Is that faith, continually being recalibrated during a life?

"That should happen daily," he said. "I die to my own death dealing with passions and choices each day so that I can live in and by the partnership, the gift of faith I am given. I seek to let that shape and inform my life.

"It comes down to our vision of God and what we think we are here for," he said. "I think we are here to reflect and embody the love of the creator of the universe so that others can know and experience the joy of that life. That life calls us into a community of partnership and friendship through faith."

Why, I asked Pastor Red, did I feel so compelled to ex-plore this idea of faith? I wasn't sure where I was going next, or who I would talk to.

"During your career as a writer, you have always tried to pursue the questions and write the stories that animate and give life meaning," he said. "For that reason alone, you are going to be drawn more deeply into that wider and deeper con-versation about who we are.

"How do I live in the world without despair?" he asked. "What are the resources? Stories help us make sense of life. On this journey of yours, you are a holy man. You are set apart.

You should embrace, with joy and gratitude, your longing to engage in the difficult questions.

"You have a great name. Thomas," Pastor Red said, "in the Bible he is called the doubter. When Jesus asked if people knew where he was going, Thomas said he didn't. After the resurrection, all were there but Thomas. Jesus shows them his hands. Thomas says that unless he sees wounds from the nails, he will not believe. The next week, behind locked doors, Jesus shows Thomas and says, do not doubt—believe.

"Thomas was only asking the questions that everyone else had," Pastor Red said. "In that sense he is the doubter, the skeptic. Where I like to see Thomas is as the one who wants to delve in deeply and not settle for some superficial explanation. The questions you ask are the ones that make a life worth living."

Less than an hour before the Sunday service, Pastor Burchfield stood before twenty-five people in a classroom to conduct the first in a series of classes exploring the Bible. He looked over adults who sat as attentively as if they were in third grade.

He was, they believed, the man with the answers.

He knew the truth.

During his career, he has led ten churches. At the first one, right out of seminary, a member approached, saying he had a question about God, Jesus Christ, and the Bible. Pastor Red had spent years preparing for this moment. Did the man want a deep analysis of the psalms? Or maybe an explanation of the link between the Old and New Testaments? Perhaps a study of Paul's role. The question was simple: Do you believe in all this shit?

Taken back, Pastor Red knew then that his life's challenge would be to help people see God's story in their own lives. And, of course, to see it in his own.

He clapped his hands.

"The Lord be with you," he told the group. "Let's pray."

When the lesson ended, he hustled from the room. He was running behind schedule and the church was filling with people who were waiting for him to impart great wisdom in the Sunday sermon.

I saw him, in that moment, as just a man grappling with the same doubts that I, too, had encountered.

That reassured me.

As he walked, nodding to members arriving at the front door, he buttoned his shirt, then reached into his pocket and pulled out the small white tab. Carefully he threaded it beneath the collar.

This boy will be a pastor.

That reassured me, too.

It's better to have a partner than go it alone.
Share the work, share the wealth.
And if one falls down, the other helps,
But if there's no one to help, tough!

Two in a bed warm each other.
Alone, you shiver all night.

By yourself you're unprotected.
With a friend you can face the worst.
Can you round up a third?
A three-stranded rope isn't easily snapped.

—Ecclesiastes 4:9–12

"This verse speaks of the value of friendship
and is special to me because I think
of the most important people in my life when I read it.
God gives us the gift of companionship.
We are not meant to walk this life alone.
With each other we discuss, doubt, celebrate, and love.
Science advances more in the spirit of collaboration
rather than in competition;
our wisdom increases as we talk and learn from each other.
God expects us to work through our struggles together,
including our questions about faith."

—*Dr. Katrina Hay*

CHAPTER 8

Faith's Equation

With each step through the college's science center, Dr. Katrina Hay left one world behind and resumed her place in the other. In one, she could prove nothing. In the other, nothing mattered but proof.

She'd spent the last three days at a Bible camp for young people. As a girl she'd attended a similar camp and later was a counselor. In college she served as the camp's director, and she felt such a deep connection to the place that she and her husband were married there.

She made her way up the steps and crossed a sprawling, open-area chemistry and physics laboratory where she helped students conduct experiments that were measured in scientific precision.

Jesus was raised from the dead?

A giant rock was moved?

If her students proposed such an experiment and didn't come back with data that could be tested and replicated, she'd fail them. But for the past few days, none of that mattered. She had been immersed in faith and God's love and surrounded by a community that believed in the power of Jesus Christ.

Returning to the camp was an annual event for Hay, who

this year led a session on astronomy. Her father was a park ranger, and Hay spent much of her childhood in a place most people would call the middle of nowhere. She loved stargazing, and astronomy had been her passion when she was younger and what drove her to learn more about science. When it came time to choose a major in college, she was torn between music and physics. She knew they seemed to be mutually exclusive, but they were daily reminders of how she approached faith.

Music is what brought her to church. Her mother, a musician, had searched for a church with the best music. As an adult, Hay came to believe that the first steps into faith can come from many directions: a search for music, a word from a stranger, or just a feeling that something seems right when a person settles into a pew.

That's what she'd tried telling the children during the Bible camp. To peer into the night sky is to be confronted with questions about life. Science, clearly, helps us understand how light makes its way to Earth. But equally as important is looking up and feeling overwhelmed—perhaps even insignificant—and open to mysteries of life and connection to a force that exists within all people. She wanted those children to see it was possible to feel spiritual and faithful far from church, hymns, and sermons.

She got as much out of the camp as did the children. Camp time, as she called it, was a place where she learned— once again—to experience faith like a child, in a way that was black and white. A child wasn't comfortable with the gray areas of life. Hay believed that if a child was given a solid foundation of faith—here is what I believe—and sent into the world, he'd learn soon enough about life's gray areas that await all of us. Faith, there, would serve as a compass to help navigate life.

She started going to church when she was eight, and it

provided a community in a small farming town. As she grew older, she had faith questions and doubts that her parents encouraged, telling her that questions had a place in a person's faith journey. Her family was open-minded about science and religion and the different roles they played in life.

That's what Hay told children at the camp. Her lesson had been that no one had to choose between faith and science. In the greater community, she knew, there could appear to be a conflict between the two. She knew of people who had fallen from faith because they felt they had to make a choice. Around a campfire, surrounded by people of faith, Hay didn't have to feel ashamed about what she believed. But now she was back in her other world.

Later that day she was scheduled to meet with a student who was conducting a series of complicated experiments involving animals and physics. Scientists were discovering that animals interact with the world in a way rooted in science. To understand why a wet dog shakes itself to effectively dry itself, one had to turn to physics, which proved why that made sense. Her student—using high-speed photography, pages of formulas, and mock-ups of animal tongues—was trying to understand why animals lapped water in certain ways.

As she approached her office, Hay created a mental list of what she expected from the student, from all her students: proof.

And then she saw the bench outside her office door. In that moment—as she unlocked her door and stepped into her office—she thought not of science, but the teachings of Jesus Christ.

Pastor Red had told me the Bible wasn't "the answer" but would serve as a guidebook to understanding God's message of love. I wanted to find a way to understand the Bible, which I saw as something mythic. Putting a hand on the Bible compelled someone to tell the truth, right? But in the discard bin at the Goodwill I could find numerous Bibles, some even signed, given in love to a child from a parent.

Annette Steele, the woman who had cleaned homes for decades, considered the Bible sacred and true. At the Van Arnam home, Tracie and her husband had an intimate relationship with the Bible, referring to specific passages as we talked about God, loss, and faith. At church, Pastor Mark Strong would ask us to stand and open our Bibles to a passage that he'd read out loud. I didn't carry a Bible. I glanced at people around me at church and found they'd marked in their Bibles, underlining passages, some pages more yellow highlight than white. Instead of being a treasured book brought out only on special occasions, these people seemed to use the Bible, not caring if the pages were wrinkled.

Back at home I picked up my Bible. Annette Steele had told me to flip through the pages, read whatever I landed on, and try to make sense of the words. That seemed similar to me picking up a guitar and trying to play jazz without mastering a simple three-chord progression.

So I began reading the Bible at the beginning. Within thirty pages, I ran into problems.

God forms man out of dirt and blows into his nostrils the breath of life?

When Adam was 130 years old he had a son?

Adam lived a total of 930 years?

Noah was 600 years old when the floodwaters covered the Earth?

An episode of the *Twilight Zone* seemed more believable. How was the Bible any different than the *Lord of the Rings*, with its Hobbits, magic ring, and talking trees? I couldn't understand how a well-educated man could believe in the Bible and, indirectly, faith. This was the part of faith that most troubled me, the sense that those of faith were sheep. Instead of critically thinking, I assumed Christians were followers who did what they were told without attempting to understand why. To call myself a Christian linked me with what seemed to be nothing more than superstitions and myths.

At the core, my question was simple: Could a so-called smart person have faith? Or was faith only possible when we accepted that we'd never have hard evidence?

If that was the case, then we were only deluding ourselves, and Christian faith had roots similar to those of the people I'd seen at festivals who bought crystals they claimed helped them navigate the world.

As much as I was drawn to faith, I'd be unable to take more than a few tentative steps on my journey until I was able to resolve this conflict.

I sat in a hard chair across from Dr. Katrina Hay, remembering what it was like to be back in college, visiting my professor during office hours. I explained my dilemma and where I was on this journey of mine. I was torn between two concepts: faith—impossible to prove—and my need for scientific proof that faith was real.

"A lot of people grapple with that," she said. "They may feel they have to choose one or the other—faith or science. But that was not a part of my childhood nor is it a part of my life now that I'm an adult."

I told her I knew next to nothing about science but science ruled so many parts of my life that I knew scientific principles were true. That wasn't the case with faith. How could the two be reconciled when scientists know that our sun is one of 100 billion stars in the Milky Way galaxy, and that galaxy is one of about 100 billion galaxies in the universe?

And somehow I'm supposed to believe that God has decided to focus all his power on us, on something smaller than a grain of sand on a miles-long beach? As a faith neophyte, I told her that I felt forced to pick one camp or the other.

"Science and faith answer different questions," she said. "I am in a profession where we observe, test, and prove. On one level, faith is one of those unanswerable questions that is impossible to test and come up with a conclusive proof. But I live faith. It's deep inside me and I'd feel empty without it."

My struggle, I told her, was that I want evidence of faith. I certainly didn't get it with Jonah Van Arnam. Even Pastor Red Burchfield—who had spent years studying theology and then a career immersed in faith—told me that he struggled with doubts. I didn't want to trust in something that couldn't be proven.

I told Hay that if we went into the woods and looked at the stars, she could tell me the scientific history of the universe in a way that made sense—even to a guy who got a D in high-school chemistry. But what moves me when I look at the stars are questions about life and meaning, questions for which there seem to be no answers.

She told me to stop being so hard on myself.

"Physics and science seek to answer and discover truths and laws that govern the physical universe," she said. "For a question to be of interest to a scientist, it must be testable. Science studies the observable universe. A physicist has to be able to make observations about it and test it. Faith on the other hand can ask these questions: Why do the physical laws exist? Is there a driving power or entity behind them? And, even deeper, what is my purpose in being here?"

She got up from behind her desk and walked to a board where she'd scribbled a series of formulas.

"Cosmology asks questions about the time line and the great scale of the universe," she explained. "A cosmologist can trace the temperatures and forces of nature back to ten to the negative forty-six seconds after the big bang. With more physics, we could go back even further in time."

She looked at me.

"But what happened before t (time) equals zero?" she asked.

I shrugged.

"A physicist will not answer that question," she said. "You could not tie a physicist down and get him or her to answer that question. We don't have any observable evidence to even begin to tackle that question. One of the things I like to say about physicists is that we're very comfortable with uncertainty. We can hold multiple possibilities of the truth on equal footing. We can hold them there for future findings to reveal the truth about them.

"Most people feel uncomfortable with that," she said. "Most people want to hear a yes or no. Is something true or not? Then they can move forward and forget about it. I think that's where you are with faith."

I agreed but said I still had a difficult time not knowing.

"Physicists are comfortable with not knowing something," she said. "I'll say that I will take the question as far as I can with the knowledge that I have. Then, when I can't go any further, I'm okay with that. This might be true and that might be true, but I can't make any judgments. Doesn't that sound like faith?"

I asked what would happen if a stranger ran into her at a party, learned of her profession, and asked her a physics question. I assumed that grabbing common tools found in any house, she could demonstrate the laws of physics in a way that would be proof. But what would happen if that stranger asked—based strictly on her profession—if she believed in God?

"That's hard," she said. "I seek that answer, too. There's nothing wrong with the searching process and asking the questions. What I want to tell you is what I tell myself: It is okay to not fully know the answer. Faith is trust. You have to step out of your comfort zone to have faith. Faith is something greater than you."

When she was in college, Hay looked for a community of students similar to herself. She checked out Christian clubs, but didn't identify with them. They advertised their belief in God but didn't go deeper, certainly not exploring the kind of faith questions she had asked and that I was now asking her. Feeling a bit lost, she felt uncomfortable calling herself a Christian in college. What brought her back to faith—on her terms—were classes in math and physics.

"I learned to see the beauty in the equations that govern the universe," she said. "That sounds cheesy, but the equations go from complex to simple and elegant. I kept having the sense that someone saw these equations before me. Not just the professors, obviously. I am not even sure how to explain this, but I felt those equations were set in motion before any of us were here to observe them."

It was possible for me to go through life never understanding a single scientific equation. It didn't make my life better or worse. But could I go through life without faith?

I told her that it was possible for me to go through life never understanding a single scientific equation. It didn't make my life better or worse. But could I go through life without faith?

"I've not picked the brains of any of my atheist friends to ask if they feel empty inside," she said. "That's how I'd feel in that position. I bump up against faith in my life in several ways. That, I think, gets to the heart of your questions and the heart of your struggle on your faith journey."

Finding faith, she explained, comes in a multitude of ways. She finds it in prayer, what she calls faith's surface. But she also bumps up against faith in observing and teaching science, and showing her students how elegant this universe is. Physics can reduce the forces that govern behavior in nature to a handful of fundamental forces. That means, in layman's terms, that a scientist, given the initial conditions, can predict what's going to happen by using either quantum theory or general relativity. In a physicist's mind, that simplicity points to an elegance in the universe because everything in the universe can be described by these simple but sophisticated laws.

"I've heard people say that Einstein himself was trying to understand the mind of God," she said. "He was trying to see how all the fundamental forces of nature were related. When I do research, I'm trying to understand—in a mathematical way that has formulas to predict behavior—the mind of God. It's like peering into this universe. Deep down it's beautiful. There was an attentiveness to detail in the creation of it. The deeper you go, the more you can learn about the majesty of it all."

That was the first time I had heard Hay mention God. I asked if science, with all the advances, will eventually prove there is a God. The answer, she told me, will always be elusive. That wasn't what I wanted to hear. But she told me that's a concept I should embrace. Trust, she said, is required to make that final step of faith. If people are presented with hard evidence, then it's easy. There's an element of challenge built into faith.

"God wants us to choose for ourselves," she said. "Once

something is made simple, or easy, we forget about it. Same with faith. Questioning and being questioned is good. Not fully understanding your faith means you are constantly thinking about it."

Help me sort it out, I asked. Put me in your head and heart. She weighed the question, a professor responding to the student's query. She began with Christ, clearly an important figure with a mystery surrounding his death.

Yet there was something so amazing that people around Christ had to tell the story, which continues to this day. The scientist in her can look to physical evidence that proves that Jesus Christ did exist. But the question Christians must confront are the circumstances surrounding the crucifixion and whether Christ, in fact, raised from the dead.

"On some level I am comforted by the questions because the questions keep me connected to God, keep me asking," she said. "As a scientist, my job is to ask questions. We can argue about things that have been tested and observations people make. But then it comes down to two questions: Do you believe there is a creator? Or do you believe the existence of this universe is a coincidence? There's nothing to prove or disprove either opinion. We can separate ourselves at that point, and that's faith."

Hay said the struggle and search are what makes faith stronger, forcing a person to think deeply about faith.

"At that point, faith becomes a journey to seek the truth," she said. "If you ever feel that you found the truth, then I feel sorry for you. Complacency in faith is like surrender. That's where faith actually holds something in common with science. Science is always about the search for truth. It is an ongoing search, process, and struggle.

"That, to me, also describes the faith journey," she said. "Since I feel comfortable with uncertainty, that carries into my faith life. I feel comfortable that I don't know. And yet enough discomfort that I still want to search for the answers.

I like the comfort and strength in people of faith, I told her, but I didn't know if I could surrender to get it. If someone would just say, here's the proof, I'd be grateful. I can't embrace faith on just emotion, but I also don't want it to be all intellectual.

"Then you will find you are not so different," she said. "You can have this passionate belief in faith and still be searching for the truth. I'm trying to find answers to everything I can find answers to, and I'm comfortable with the questions that have no answers. When I dig to a point where I don't have an answer, I have to let the answer come from the heart. Then you become vulnerable. When you're vulnerable, you are more in touch with yourself."

I followed Hay as she left her office to check on the student conducting the experiment in a small lab. She studied his figures in a logbook, examined a contraption he'd constructed to simulate a cat's tongue in action, and then peered over his shoulder as he ran a computer program putting it all together.

None of it made sense to me, but Hay was satisfied, offered him an encouraging word, and returned to her office.

I asked her what she was thinking about. She told me the Bible camp. She'd been moved—almost to tears—when the young people revealed to her what they worried about: divorced parents, drugs, and relationships. What could she say to help?

"Jesus is always there," she said. "The light shines in the darkness and the darkness can't overcome the light. Jesus is the light, with the power to heal and guide through compassion and patience."

As she approached her office, Hay saw the wooden bench that reminded her that faith is real.

"I had come to my office one night and saw a student sitting on that bench," she said, pausing to run her hand over the wood. "She said she needed help with her homework. The girl wasn't in my class and it wasn't my official office hour.

"I went into my office and shut the door," Hay told me. "I was frustrated that she was there, and I wanted to send her a signal that I was busy and she should leave. I was in my office, surrounded by all my scientific books and periodicals, when I felt the presence of Jesus in that room. Compassion and patience were a part of his teachings. Was I living up to the faith that I believed?"

Finally, she opened the door, walked to the bench, and sat next to the girl. The problem was difficult. Even with Hay's help, it took the student more than thirty minutes to solve it.

"That was the last interaction I had with her," Hay said. "She died in a hiking accident."

Hay led the way back into her office and took a seat behind her desk.

"Faith and science," she told me, "seek simplicity in a complex world."

Before leaving her office, I asked her about one of the formulas she'd scrawled on a board. She pushed away from her desk, walked to the board, and picked what she said was the simplest one: $F=MA=0$.

"It means that every force acting on an object affects its behavior," Hay said.

At that moment, Hay was talking about "F" in terms of gravity.

I, though, was thinking that "F" was something altogether quite different.

But Jacob stayed behind by himself,
and a man wrestled with him until daybreak.
When the man saw that he couldn't get the best of Jacob
as they wrestled, he deliberately threw Jacob's hip out of joint.
The man said, "Let me go; it's daybreak."
Jacob said, "I'm not letting you go 'til you bless me."
The man said, "What's your name?"
He answered, "Jacob."
The man said, "But no longer. Your name is no longer Jacob.
From now on it's Israel (God-Wrestler);
you've wrestled with God and you've come through."

—Genesis 32:24–28

"Man, for me, this is it.
In so many ways, you must wrestle to truly
find your character and faith."

—Mitch Coats

CHAPTER 9

Faith's Warrior

All his life, Mitch Coats wanted to test himself against the best in the world. The black belt he'd earned in Brazilian jujitsu was one of his most prized possessions, awarded only after years of hard work, injuries, and blood spilled on the mat. He'd won plenty of competitions, but the best would be assembling at the annual Master's event in Brazil, the birthplace of his chosen martial art, and Coats wanted to travel from Boise, Idaho, to participate.

He prayed on the matter, seeking God's guidance and support for what he knew would be a struggle to save up the money, continue running his dojo—his martial arts school—and pay for his living expenses. He ran it by his wife. She supported him. They sat down with a budget and agreed to give up date nights, movies, and eating out. Slowly—with ten- and twenty-dollar deposits—the account grew.

Coats prayed, thanking God for making his dream come true. People who didn't know Coats would be surprised that he thought of God, let alone prayed. Faith was a side of himself he kept hidden because he approached it so differently. He didn't go to church, wasn't into singing, sitting still, or listening to sermons.

From a distance, he looked like one of those guys who

preachers warn boys to stay away from. Here comes trouble. In a past life, they'd have been right. Both his arms were covered with full-sleeve tattoos running from his shoulder to his wrist. The ink was a reminder that Coats was once a hellion who beat up people for fun.

He changed—not through church and someone nagging at him to find God and turn his life around, but through fighting.

He read the Bible daily and conducted himself in ways he believed showed he was as faithful as anyone who sat in a pew come Sunday.

Now, after all those years of sacrifice, it was his time to shine in Brazil. He thanked God.

Two weeks before it was time to leave, Coats was working out with a handful of his advanced students who were planning to compete in lower divisions. He twisted, working on an advanced move he'd need to work perfectly if he had a chance of earning a medal in Brazil, when he heard something pop.

Pain shot through his body.

He lay back on the mat and struggled to breathe. He pulled open his gi—his jujitsu uniform—and knew he was in trouble. One of his bottom ribs looked ready to poke through his skin. After a trip to the hospital, he was sent home. Brazil was out. He was told to stay in bed.

He wallowed in pity for three days.

It had been his time.

He deserved it.

In 1999, for the second time in my career, I was a Pulitzer Prize finalist, and I was sure I had a winner.

It was my time.

I deserved it.

The way the contest works is that newspapers around the country enter what they consider their best work in various categories—feature stories, for example—and a group of jurors selects the best three, which are considered Pulitzer Finalists. Those three stories are sent to the Pulitzer Board, which picks the winner.

I'd written a powerful story about a man who'd worked as a claims analyst for a health insurance company. He'd come home from church when his mother invited him to come to her house for lunch. On the way there, a car slammed into the side of his car. His heart stopped twice. He remained in a coma for a week, and didn't speak for two months. He had to be taught how to swallow and control his bowels. He wore a diaper for two months.

He suffered a brain injury and had such severe memory loss that he had to use Post-it notes throughout his apartment to remind himself to do the simplest things: turn off the light, make sure the stove is off, and lock the door. Two years after the wreck, the health company hired him back—as a janitor. Strangers thought he was retarded or stupid. Over time he became a loner. I spent months following this man as he rebuilt his life.

As great as I considered the story, it didn't win the prize and I fell into a funk. I spent the next three months doing a lot of soul searching: Why did I so badly want the Pulitzer? Did my writing fail me? What did I do wrong? Why were these awards—and I had won all of them but the Pulitzer—so important to me?

I took stock of myself, both the good and the bad. I let some things go and embraced others. At the end of that self-exploration, I discovered two things: Awards didn't matter as much as I thought they did. What I loved was a good story.

Two months later, the telephone at my desk rang. A man

on the other end of the line told me he'd read my stories over the years and he wanted to tell me about a Portland family with a story. They'd never talked about it, but if they did, I would be the one to tell their story. Two years later, that story won the Pulitzer Prize for Feature Writing.

Now I saw a parallel with my faith journey. I couldn't rush this process, or decide a time line. All I could do was be aware of the people of faith who God put in my life. I had to wait for the symbolic phone to ring. But I also had to let people know what I was seeking. If I mentioned Jesus Christ and God in conversations—not preaching, but inquiring—I found some people had such strong reactions, good and bad, to the words that it led to more of a debate than a meaningful conversation.

It made me think about the difference between karate and aikido. Karate is a clash of power. Aikido is about blending with your opponent's strength. The second approach seemed appropriate now. At a party or around strangers, I could bring up faith and engage people in a conversation, starting at the edges and slowly making my way to the heart of the matter, which was God. Some people's faith surprised me: a grizzled biker, a musician, and one of the wealthiest businessmen I've ever met.

Duncan Campbell talked about his faith only when I casually mentioned that I'd been going to a church to learn about faith and prayer. His parents were emotionally abusive alcoholics. As a child, they'd leave him at home and go to a bar. He was so lonely and neglected that something died within him. He acted out and was suspended from elementary school.

When he was eight, he talked a friend of his into going to a church down the street. It wasn't about God at that point. Campbell just wanted company. As he grew older, he became an overachiever who wanted to make something out of his life. A logical, evidence-based man, he no longer thought about

God. If anything, he was mad at God: Where had He been for me? What kind of God gives a kid the kind of childhood and the parents he'd had?

"In time I developed a successful company that manages timberland for investors," he told me. "One evening my wife and I were at a dinner party, and a man at the table started talking about his faith in Jesus. I said religion was a crutch. He didn't argue. He invited me to come to his small-group Bible study. I agreed for my own reasons: I still liked meeting people, and attending might be stimulating and interesting."

"I went to that small group for two years and I found myself warming to the idea of God," he said. "I even started attending church. The pastor said my flirtation with God was like falling in love, getting engaged, but never getting married. I was on an airplane home after a business trip and suddenly I felt this tug on my heart that I needed to make it official. I needed to come to God. Finally, all my arguments fell away and I asked Christ into my life, and He became the foundation of my faith."

In time he learned why God gave him the childhood he did—so he could mentor kids who were vulnerable like he'd been. Using his own money, he started Friends of the Children, an innovative program that has changed the lives of more than 750 children in cities across the United States by assigning a paid mentor for at-risk kids. The mentor meets with the child at least once a week from first grade through high school.

"I know the lives those kids lead because I had been one," he told me. "Jesus said, *'Let the little children come to me, and do not hinder them'* [Matthew 19:14]. We nurture and care for kids with the unconditional love of Christ."

Hearing Campbell's story reminded me that I had to follow my heart, just the way I did when I reported a story.

What interested me? Could I find God there?

All my life I've been intrigued by fighters, mixed martial arts, and boxing. My wife doesn't get it, and sees the sports as brutal. She gets no argument from me, but I've tried explaining to her that a man discovers himself not on the golf course, but in the ring, facing a skilled opponent who wants to hurt him. There are no teammates and you can't hide. It's a place where doubt and fear collide, a place where a man discovers what he's made of.

It reminded me of faith.

I told Mitch Coats that most people who ran into him would be worried he'd beat them up if they said something to annoy him. No one would ever think he was a man of faith. He chuckled and told me that he didn't have much use for what would be considered organized religion.

"I was raised in a church and even baptized there when I was a kid," he said. "But honestly, faith wasn't something I thought a lot about as a kid. I think it's hard for a child to be able to make a conscious choice about God and faith. I had two profound events in my life. One that pushed me away from faith. The other brought me back to it.

"When I was eleven my parents got divorced and everything in my life turned upside down," he said. "My mom had me involved in church then and the pastor was like, you know, trying to be sympathetic in that Christian way. Even as a young kid, I knew B.S. when I encountered it. I asked him if his parents were divorced. He said no. I asked him how he could help me. He had no idea where I was coming from."

Coats quit going to church because the people there were trying to preach and counsel him, but they had no real-world experience.

"I'd lived a life of hard knocks," he said. "I couldn't identify with them. I felt distant from religion and faith because I was different. There wasn't a place for me in faith the way I knew faith. Eventually I started going to a few services, but man got in the way of it. Not any one man. I mean man—the human race.

"I feel like man is flawed," he said. "I'm flawed. You're flawed. We don't want to admit that to each other, so we judge others, acting like we're better than they are. My struggle, if you want to know the truth, was being around judgmental people in the faith. If you spend any time in a church or around people who claim to be faithful, you've run into them.

"There is pure faith," he said. "And then there is this faith where people think they are better than other people because they have it. For someone like me, struggling enough with life, I didn't need that. I was hard enough on myself. I had no understanding of faith. I wasn't the kind of guy to go looking for an answer."

He drifted away, praying from time to time, but his heart wasn't in it. Prayer was more of a habit left over from when he was a kid. The way he was living and thinking—rough around the edges—didn't leave much room for God. He came back to faith in a roundabout way that had nothing to do with church, the Bible, or God.

"What changed in my life was my first jujitsu instructor," he said. "He died from brain cancer. He was thirty-four and left behind two kids. That man was my moral compass in life. He was the person who held me accountable to do the right thing. He introduced me to the true meaning of faith. Then he died. I lost it. I didn't care about anything in life."

Listening to his story, I felt a sense of hope, a reminder that people come to faith at different times in their lives and in different ways. And it's possible to fall away, but come back simply by trusting the guide.

"That's what's wonderful about faith," Coats said. "So here's my life now. I read the Bible and pray. I don't go to church because I haven't found one that speaks to me and what I need. Some people might say I don't have faith because they look at the trappings of faith.

"Forget that," he said. "I have faith. What I know, and what I'm certain of, is that faith is not dependent on a church. You know where I found my way back to God and my faith? All the way in Thailand. When I think about it, it's crazy. But cool, too.

"My real journey in faith began because of the martial arts and my jujitsu instructor," Coats said. "His name was Dean and his death was profound. But he left behind a gift for me and that was this faith journey. He dies and I find this new life.

"Before he died he sat me down and said he had cancer," he said. "That's a serious opponent. He told me that he'd been fighting melanoma since he was twenty-six. He'd undergone eleven major surgeries. This was a strong, tough man. I asked him how he held up. He told me that his faith kept him strong. He'd outlasted all the doctor's predications of how long he'd live. When I heard that stuff about faith, I started to think about what faith was in the real world."

Coats told me that Dean was a good Christian, but also a man he could respect. Coats needed to hear faith's message from a man who was tough and who could beat him up if he wanted to.

"I think we all have someone out there who gets our respect, our ear, and then our heart when it comes to faith," he said. "The man I listen to does nothing for you. That's okay. The person who starts you on your faith journey isn't the right one for me. You like the choir? Not for me. Being tough was a big deal for me.

"When I was young, I never really lost a fight," he said. "I've been in a ton of them. I was never humbled. Dean humbled me. He was a fantastic fighter. He whipped me. What he taught me was humility. Until you get your bubble burst, you never really understand humility. It's not just a word. It's a state of mind, a place where you are broken. Once Dean broke me down, he built me back up. That's what God does through our trials and tribulations. In my case, God worked through Dean."

Listening to him made me think of Annette Steele and how she'd come into my life through story, which was as central to who I was as fighting was to Coats, and science, to Dr. Katrina Hay. I wondered if along the way other people had been there for me, but I'd missed them because I wasn't ready.

"Dean had a few tattoos and a child before he got married," he said. "He wasn't perfect. The most important thing I've learned is that our role models in faith don't have to be perfect. When we think about our flaws, we feel we're not men of faith or even worthy to be in faith. There's this crazy idea that you have to be perfect. And, man, I was far from perfect.

"I ended up moving to another state to train," he said. "Everything was going great. Then Dean called one night with this bad news. The cancer had spread to his brain. He was starting to lose his way. He couldn't really drive anymore, and his life was slipping away. I faced a tough choice. I was on track to do what I wanted with my life.

"It was my time," he said. "But I'd been doing a lot of thinking about Dean's faith and what I learned—and what I could learn—from him. So I quit my job, quit training, and came back to live with my father and be around Dean. I helped Dean do everything: go to the bathroom and get in bed. I hung out with him. He spent time in the hospital before he ended up in hospice. I spent nights in the hospital with him."

In the hospital, Coats immersed himself in the reality of faith. Dean talked to him about God and prayed with him. Dean told Coats to read the book of Proverbs and contemplate how it applied to his life. When Coats read a proverb, Dean had Coats tell him what he thought it meant in the real world.

"He was about as far away from a pastor as you could get, but we'd have these discussions that went from Proverbs to my life to faith and how everything was wrapped up together," he said. "What Dean did was engage me with faith. You see, I was raised by my dad, and there wasn't a lot of sharing of feelings. He asked me how I felt about faith. Dean, this tough guy, was like my minister."

When I went to that church on assignment for the newspaper, it wasn't the pastor who engaged me. It was a stranger who gave me a squeeze on the shoulder when he walked back to his seat. His vulnerability drew me in.

"This was a tough guy and a man I respected," Coats said. "So when he pushed me to reveal what I was feeling, I did it. With someone else, a pastor? Don't think so. Like I said, God puts the right person in our lives at the right time for the faith journey. A guy like me needed someone who could take me down in a heartbeat. So here we are, two tough guys," he said. "We had a relationship that I know some people looked at as kind of weird. We're doing all this praying and talking about feelings. Since he had all these surgeries, he was jacked up with scars. Before he ended up in the hospice, I'd give him massages to relieve his pain. I bet it seemed weird to see me rubbing some guy. I didn't care."

Coats said that Dean taught him the most important lesson: you don't have to be a pushover or weakling to say you believe in the Lord and have faith.

As Dean's protégé and most dedicated student, Coats was asked to be a pallbearer at the funeral. More than three hundred people came to the church, and Coats saw all parts of Dean's life on display: work clique, jujitsu, and church, where he also volunteered. Coats wanted to have a similar impact on the world.

"What I most liked was Dean's imperfections," he said. "The child he had was from a one-night-stand thing, and the baby was given up for adoption. But Dean tried to do the right thing even after he got married to another woman who was a schoolteacher. They had two kids. But Dean never forgot that baby. He didn't go at it hard. He wanted her to have her own family, but he never forgot her.

"He ruled my world with an iron fist," Coats said. "He smashed me many times. I got to see the soft and strong sides of faith. Here was a man so tender about his little girl, and then he was the toughest guy I ever knew.

"God put him in my life to show me about faith and what it means in a life," he said. "When I first met Dean, I was a kid with a big ego. I was bouncing in bars and beating guys up. I thought I was the toughest guy that ever walked. Then I walked into Dean's class and he humbled me.

"I left and wanted to come back and beat him," he said. "He humbled me again. This went on for two weeks. I said okay, I have to learn that. He later told me that when I came in to his class, he hated me. He wanted to beat me up so bad that I'd leave. When I kept coming, he realized he had to invest some time in me."

That sounds so much like our relationship with God. Do you think that we need to be humbled, especially men?

"Yes," he said. "Obviously people search for something in time of need. When you pray, you basically break down. You bend over, get on your knees, and get in a passive position.

Same with training and fighting. No one is good at fighting right away. You have to learn from experience and hard knocks.

"There are two types of people in the martial arts," he said. "You get the guy who comes in the first day and is not as tough as he thinks he is. He walks away and pretends it never happened. You never see him again. Or you get the guy who admits he feels helpless. That helpless feeling is what motivates the guy to learn.

"It's the same way with faith," he said. "Everyone knows it's out there. Some people have a stronger faith, but I don't think there's anyone alive who hasn't experienced at least a hint of faith. Everyone has had a faith lesson. What do we do with that lesson? Do we study it? Or do we walk away from it and pretend it never happened?"

When he was younger, Coats wanted to beat his opponent physically and emotionally and make a man crumble. Faith softened his heart. He realized when a guy was drunk or not in shape. Coats knew he had power over people who don't realize what could happen to them.

"At that moment I started to give back to people," he said. "I now try to live as an example for my martial arts students. I'm happily married. I give to charity, I try to do things as in the Bible. I fail, of course. But faith reminds me each day that there's a purpose for me that's bigger than my ego and more important than what I want for me.

"I had to go through those problems in life," he said. "I had to go through those trials. But don't we all? I was exposed to religion and faith as a young kid. I left it, but came back to faith on my own terms. That's what's so important. The faith journey is about rediscovering faith when falling away, and redefining what faith is at that time in your life. Faith is not a concept. Faith is alive.

From the outside, I told Coats, it seemed that faith and fighting were similar.

"Yes, and here's why," he said. "You get humbled in the presence of something you don't really understand. When you start a martial art, you don't really understand what's happening to you. You wonder how you are going to survive it. But you do. Then you become more skilled.

Faith and fighting are similar . . . "and here's why," he said. "You get humbled in the presence of something you don't really understand.

"In faith you're not sure whether you're worthy to do this," he said. "Am I doing the right thing? Am I reading the right scripture? You're not sure what's going on. Martial arts training and faith training are the same thing. You have to take the time to do it. I spend thirty minutes a day reading Scripture. I pray once a day, in the shower. I get on my knees. No one sees me. It's the same as fighting. I make time to train to better myself.

"I study the Bible," he said. "I flip through it and stop on something. I try and read a story passage or verse and let it guide me. I don't know every story in the Bible, and I'm not good with quoting verses. I like Proverbs and Psalms. I like things that make me reflect on faith and my life more than just hearing a story.

He said his faith gives him a softness that complements his strength. His grandfather was a champion boxer in the U.S. Navy, and his father earned a black belt in kung fu. Coats comes from a long line of fighters, but he wasn't raised with affection. At his martial arts school he's affectionate with his students. He hugs them and asks what's going on in their lives.

"But I also kick the crap out of them," he said. "I can't

force faith or religion on people. I don't want to push it. Do I know that Jesus walked the Earth? Yes, one hundred percent. Do I know that He is the son of God and resurrected? Sometimes I struggle with that. Is it real? But do I feel like I have something to learn from that guy? Yes.

"I'm on my own faith journey," he said. "I'm not blindly following like I'm a sheep. I've seen things that some people haven't. I've had life experiences that some people haven't. How the hell would you know what I've gone through?

"Sometimes people who are pushy about faith talk out of their butt," he said. "These are people that live a charmed life. They've never kicked someone in the teeth when they're down. How can I connect with these guys? That was my biggest issue. Yeah, I had an inkling of faith, but it didn't seem to have any place in my life and the kind of man I was. That's why Dean was so important."

I thought back to some of the teachers I'd had in school. Some—even as far back as sixth grade—had a profound impact on the course of my life in what, at the time, had seemed minor ways. Does God present us with the right teacher at the right time? Did God place Dean in Mitch's life?

"You bet," he said. "And after I learned all those lessons from him, after feeling I've found the man who will help me on my path, he dies. I was rocked. Out of the blue one of my friends gave me a ticket to go backpacking in Thailand.

"When I'm there, everyone keeps asking me if I'm going to see the mummy," he said. "One day I had some time and I went to see what everyone was talking about. I walked through the woods on an elephant trail. There, in the middle of the woods, is this temple, all ornate with a little glass case with this monk who was enshrined in it.

"The plaque said that he so loved his congregation of followers that he wanted to show the power of God to them," he said. "He fasted and meditated and mummified himself when it was time to die. His skin was all there. He had his robe on and was sitting in an Indian-style position. That was my epiphany. I realized that I had to believe in something.

"Dean was gone," he said. "But that didn't mean that my faith had to end. A life without faith is an empty place to be. We, as people, need to believe in something. I pray before I compete or fight. It's a scary proposition knowing you're going into combat against another man. No matter how tough you are, you're always scared. But your fears save you. The prayer is the same: God, I am your soldier, and I know you have a plan for me.

"I don't pray to win," he said. "I pray to be brave and be a soldier of God. The Bible is rife with battles and good versus evils and defeats and triumphs. When someone sits there and calls faith soft, I ask them if they've read the Bible."

On the inside of his gi, Coats has written "RIP Dean." It's a reminder that the man made an impact on his life. If a person leads a good life and affects another person and they pass it on to someone else, that's eternal life. Once Coats was a jerk. He now has eighty-five students who look up to him.

"I'm a soldier of God," he said. "That's the tough side of faith. The soft side is realizing that at some point, someone is always looking at you and what you do. I'm not embarrassed to say I have faith. My faith reveals parts of me that seem to be hidden from the world. In faith, we see our humanity with each other.

"When I think about God and faith, I remember the person who was my godfather when I was a kid," he said. "He was the Sunday school teacher. All those years, he kept in touch with me. He'd send me a birthday card every year. I never wrote back. Finally, after about ten years, I did.

"Like God, he showed me that you don't give up on people," he said. "Really, you don't give up on yourself. Maybe I'll have the honor of being the Dean in someone's life."

Mitch Coats allowed himself a few days of self-pity while lying in bed and recovering from the injury that had ended his dream of competing in Brazil.

He prayed and asked God for guidance. He remembered Dean and thought about how he would handle the setback.

And then he made his decision: he would go to Brazil.

Not as a competitor, but as a coach and cheerleader for his students who were competing.

It was their time.

Become wise by walking with the wise;
hang out with fools and watch your life
fall to pieces.

—Proverbs 13:20

"I fought everything tooth and nail
And then Ms. Mary came into my life."

—*Jill K. Smith*

CHAPTER 10

A Stranger's Gift

With her husband out of town, Jill Smith worried about whether he should have set out on his own. She was a planner and thinker, and Fred's decision to leave a high-profile and secure job with the federal government in Washington, D.C., and become a management consultant weighed heavily on her mind.

Even though her husband was smart, capable, and well connected, Smith didn't like risk. She analyzed and plotted, worked the angles, and weighed her options before making a move. If life was a game, Smith approached it with the tenacity of a chess player.

The telephone rang that evening and she felt relieved to hear Fred's voice. She was anxious for him to return home and bring some semblance of calm back into their lives. He'd managed to snag his first client—a great sign, he'd told his wife—and had flown to New Orleans. Her husband filled her in on life in the city, much of it still reeling from the impact of Hurricane Katrina. Fred said that entire sections of the city were in ruins, and people were scared and battling despair. Between work and being in the center of one of the nation's biggest natural disasters, Fred was worn out.

"I don't feel well," he told his wife. "I'm exhausted."

Smith figured it must the stress of being on the road, fretting about making a good impression with the client, and feeling the pressure of being his own boss.

"Hurry home," Smith told him. "You'll feel better when you're with me."

He laughed.

"See you soon," he replied. "I love you."

Theirs had been a whirlwind romance, like in a movie where it's clear to the audience that two people are made for each other. They were smart, college educated, and ambitious. They discussed current events and ideas. While dating, their idea of a perfect Sunday was to have brunch, read the paper, and watch *Meet the Press*.

Then this boyfriend—the man she wanted to spend the rest of her life with—dropped a bombshell. He wanted to go to church. What about their Sunday ritual? He understood. Still, he wanted to go to church.

Wasting a Sunday—that's what going to church symbolized to Smith—wasn't what she had in mind. Religion had once been a part of her life. That was the key word—*once*. She'd outgrown her childhood religion. She grew up in the South in the Bible Belt. Her grandfather had been a preacher—Smith had vague memories of going to church to hear him speak—and her mother listened to gospel music while cleaning the house. Where she grew up, no one questioned God's existence. Everyone called themselves a Christian and attended church. Smith knew plenty of Bible stories, but made no connection between them and God and faith.

In college she wised up. She had questions that no one could answer. The way she'd been raised, with the heavy and oppressive church presence throughout the community, was too much for her and she became an agnostic.

She studied Buddhist philosophies and found them helpful as a way to accept what was happening and had happened in her life. When she was fourteen, her eleven-year-old brother drowned. The father figure in her life also died when she was in her teens. Those Bible stories had been of no help in sorting out the tragedies.

When her boyfriend said he wanted to go to church, it touched a nerve. It was like a teetotaler reeling in the woman, winning her heart, and then admitting he has a problem with booze. But she loved this man. A good girlfriend should go to church. Plus she didn't want to lose this guy over something as silly as a church. She asked about the place. He described it as a little church started by his friend, a guy he'd known from high school.

How little?

Well, it began with seven people meeting in someone's house.

You're serious?

Fred assured her that the church had since grown. The congregation was now large enough to meet in a room at the nearby film institute center.

Smith—always a woman who spoke her mind—said the group sounded like a cult.

And why did his friend have to create a new church with all these churches around?

And why was he so interested in church all of a sudden?

A vision, her husband said. His friend had a vision.

That was too much for Smith. She couldn't believe she was hearing this from a man so smart and rooted in the real world.

A vision? You have to be kidding.

Her boyfriend was adamant. He wanted to go to church to support his friend, but wouldn't make her go. Out of a growing love, though, she gave in. The church was nondenominational and the pastor, she learned, had a real job as a management consultant. He used PowerPoint and a big screen to get his message across to the congregation. It wasn't like the church Smith attended as a girl.

The problem was the charismatic preaching and melodrama, both of which she thought were nuts. People raised their hands during worship, talking about praising Jesus and singing and dancing to the music. Not only did she not understand what, exactly, they were praising, she felt self-conscious. Members also liked to say "I thought the Lord said . . ."

On the way home from church, when she could be watching *Meet the Press*, she argued with her boyfriend. She was sick of people claiming they heard the Lord speak. The Lord, she told her boyfriend, isn't speaking to them, thinking about them, or taking personal interest in a group of people meeting in a room in a film center.

Her boyfriend thought otherwise.

And she was going to marry this man?

She continued to attend, but remained frustrated. She married Fred, and life—other than this church nonsense—was good.

Fred arrived home from New Orleans and told his wife he felt terrible. The next morning he saw a doctor, who diagnosed swollen lymph nodes and sent him home with antibiotics. That night his temperature soared, and his wife took him to the community hospital. No one knew what was wrong. Three days later, on the advice of friends, Smith had him transferred to Georgetown University Hospital, where he ended up in the intensive care unit. Smith didn't know what to do or where to turn.

One morning, the doorbell rang.
And there stood Ms. Mary.

My family got used to me leaving each Sunday for church. Sometimes, on the way, I'd stop at a coffee shop. I felt strange when I stepped into a place full of people hanging out and reading the paper. A man in a suit and tie on a Sunday morning meant only one thing—church clothes. That's where I was going, but I didn't want to advertise it. Even though I wasn't wearing a cross or carrying a Bible, I knew that people guessed what I was up to.

What did going to church mean to them? And why did I feel somewhat embarrassed?

Back in my car, drinking my coffee with one hand and steering with the other, I'd try to analyze the situation, but couldn't come up with an answer that made sense. Only when I got within a few blocks of Life Change Christian did I quit the pondering. After parking my car, I'd walk to the church's front door, where I'd be greeted with hugs from the men who monitored the parking lot and helped the women from their cars.

Inside, the choir would be singing, and I'd lose myself in those voices. The songs were a part of it, but what stirred me were the voices—the humanity that broke through my outer shell, touched my heart, and connected me to the power of faith. By the time services ended, I'd leave church—hugging the guys in the lot on the way out—sold on the idea of faith. I felt like I'd had this incredible workout, and a runner's high carried me to my car.

On Monday, things changed. *Foolish* would be too strong a word, but as I prepared for work, paid bills, and did all that goes with being a husband and father trying to make it in the world, my intellect took over. So many people I knew considered faith a myth clung to by weak people. By midweek, I'd be back to my own life and way of doing things. Come Sunday, the cycle started again.

Over time, the choir and the songs became symbols of my faith struggle. I loved the emotion contained in a song, the beauty and power of voices melding into one. The lyrics were displayed on a large screen in front of the church. I play guitar, so I could hear the chord changes and the different tempos.

But when it was time to sing, I'd simply stand, unable to open my mouth and even whisper words that I knew would be drowned out by the voices of all those around me. Besides, who was watching and judging me? I was. I could not let myself go.

I knew that I'd never understand faith if I couldn't unblock myself. When I'd take guitar lessons, my teacher would tell me to play "emotional" or "angry," improvising while he laid down the rhythm and chord progression. I knew the scales, could play them backward and forward. But I couldn't—or wouldn't—let myself be vulnerable enough to let the music express what was in my heart.

Now I was having the same problem with faith.

Jill Smith understood my predicament, and I'd finally met someone who had also been reluctant to plunge straight into faith without analyzing why it was necessary. When people consider themselves educated, they apply that rigorous standard to all areas of their life. In the United States, we both agreed, a successful person is one who gets ahead on ability.

"So when you rely on a superpower, the supernatural, it seems like it's a weakness," she said. "You are just going to trust in God and not yourself? It doesn't make rational sense."

But her decision to go to church, I told her, grew out of something exclusively emotional—she found a man she wanted to marry.

"True," she said with a laugh. Then she turned serious and explained that even then, she approached church as if it were an intellectual exercise.

"If all this stuff about God and Jesus were true, it wouldn't hurt anyone," she said. "It was probably a good thing to go to church. If we ended up having a baby, I thought it would be good to have the child raised in a Christian family."

Since faith is so personal, I asked, how do couples come to an agreement about what role it should play in their lives?

My wife grew up in a Lutheran church. She attended each Sunday, was confirmed there, and the church played a central role in her family's life, both spiritually and emotionally. By the time she was nineteen, though, she'd drifted away, as had nearly all of the young people she'd grown up with in that church. And then here I come, in my fifties, with no church background, and I feel drawn to faith and church. That could be confusing and unsettling to a spouse.

"The relationship I had with Fred was based on talking and being good friends," she said. "My personality is that I think things through. He was in a different place in his faith walk. He's five years older than me with different experiences. He had his crisis of faith earlier in his life and reconciled it.

"I was questioning," she said. "That's a good and important part of the journey. It makes faith personal for you. You're doing this not because your family went to church, or your family believes in God or expresses faith."

That questioning, she told me, continued at church and, later, after she and Fred married.

"The parts of church I liked were the moral things," she said. "We should try and be good people and be a good example of a well-lived life. That's different than saying the Lord speaks to you and throwing your hands in the air."

Smith continued to attend because she felt the pastor was an intellectually trustworthy person. Also, the people at the church were professionals who she could see being friends with outside of church.

"Everything was good except the part that I would call, from back in the day, little Jesus freaks," she said. "They were just weird with all the hand raising. I could not get the emotional piece. I knew they believed what they believed, and I respected their right to do that. I thought they were—it sounds terrible—weak for needing faith. They need to believe this because they weren't using their brain.

> **"I thought they were— it sounds terrible— weak for needing faith."**

"I need to be able to compartmentalize and see how things are relevant," she said. "I need to believe that the person I'm listening to is smart and not just a guy off the street who had a word from the Lord."

Smith, after hearing my story, told me that she felt I was at a crossroads, of sorts, one so familiar to her. At some point— no matter how a person grows up—faith has to be a choice.

"Religion was part of my culture growing up," she said. "I had no choice. But for faith to really become personal for you, there has to be some impetus. I went through a period of contemplating. I needed the intellectual understanding of faith. I needed to study. That's the way faith initially reached me. But without a crisis, I never would have reached the other piece of faith.

"Unfortunately for most people it takes a crisis to get to

that point," she said. "You don't lose weight until the doctor tells you you're going to get diabetes. Some people don't need a wake-up call. Some do. I was one of those people."

That's when Ms. Mary came into her life.

When I heard her story, I thought of Annette Steele, the Portland cleaning woman I'd written about. The similarities between Annette and Ms. Mary were striking. Ms. Mary—what everyone called her—cleaned homes. A friend of Fred's recommended her when Fred said he and his wife were looking for help with the house. She lived ninety minutes away, but insisted that wasn't too far, and an appointment was made to meet.

"She came the first day and said she was going to adopt us as her children," Smith said. "She was short, seventy-two, and a spitfire. My husband and I wondered if we should be having some old black lady cleaning our home. Something about it seemed like she had enough in life already. We were conflicted. But this was how she made money. She saw it as her ministry. She talked about her faith. When she first came to our house, she said, 'I hope you don't mind, but every house I clean, I like to anoint with oil.'"

Smith laughed.

"You kind of expect that from a little old black lady who loves the Lord," she said. "It was a stereotypical thing. If you were to ask any black person what a seventy-two-year-old black church lady would be like, that would be Ms. Mary.

"Culturally I'm used to that figure," Smith said. "Her character type was very dominant in the African American community. She was the old grandma, your auntie. Comedians make jokes about this archetype. Ms. Mary embodied all that. She was the old black lady who goes to church all the time, wants to pray with you, and talks about the Lord.

"She was so sweet," Smith said. "I didn't care if she

wanted to anoint the house with oil. Back to the intellectual thing for me. It didn't hurt anyone if she wanted to be like that. It just wasn't me."

Ms. Mary became part of the household, showing up every other Tuesday to clean the home and keep an eye on her "kids." When Fred got sick, Smith forgot to tell Ms. Mary not to come that Tuesday.

The doorbell rang, and there stood Ms. Mary.

Smith was about to send her away, but suddenly felt that she needed to unburden her heart. She'd been immersed in the medical world, learning about blood draws and scans, but what she wanted was someone to listen to her fears. She invited Ms. Mary into the house, insisting she'd be paid for her time, and confided in the older woman, laying out all that was happening: Fred's organs were shutting down, he was on a ventilator, and the doctors warned he could die.

Ms. Mary took Smith's hand in hers. In a firm voice, she said she was on a church prayer team, and the group would immediately start praying for Fred. The best medical minds were working the case, and this cleaning woman offered only prayer, which Smith considered useless.

Days later, the doorbell rang and Ms. Mary stood outside clutching a yellow folder containing twelve pages of prayers and Bible phrases she'd typed out. She handed Smith the folder and told her it was time for her to pray for Fred.

"I said I'd do anything," Smith said. "She told me to pray and believe in God. I told her I didn't know how to pray, and I was unsure about faith. She told me to read the prayers out loud when I visited my husband. Through prayer, she said, I'd discover faith."

In the meantime, people from the church—people Smith had considered strange and weak—rallied, telling her they were praying for the couple at church. One evening Smith spotted the yellow folder, carried it into another room, and opened it. She picked up the first prayer and read it.

"I felt I owed it to Ms. Mary because she took the time to type them up," she said. "I did that for two days, just reading those prayers she gave me. On the third day, I felt something working in me. I couldn't explain it. Something opened up in me."

No longer was faith an intellectual concept to be analyzed.

"I started adding my own prayers," Smith said. "The words and Bible passages were so powerful that I started to believe them. *God, you said in your Word. I am holding you to your Word. I need you to change my situation now.* One day I asked God to help me figure out what was wrong with Fred.

"The next day, I spotted a rash on my husband's skin," she said. "It was hard to see with his very dark color. I pointed it out to the doctors. They discovered he had an infectious disease causing septic shock. The doctors gave him the right combination of antibiotics and he recovered."

What, I asked, was the meaning in this story?

"I felt faith and believed," she said. "I finally understood what all the Bible verses I'd heard all my life meant. Something changed in me. Faith is just talking to God. Sometimes it's asking Him for something. Sometimes it's thanking Him. Faith is comforting and empowering. In faith, I feel protected. Believing in God is a leap of faith. Once you access God, you treat God like He is a friend and you talk to Him throughout the day."

Smith had something else to admit.

"I lift my hands in church now," she said. "It's a physical manifestation of me opening myself up to God. We don't want to do that in front of people because it's a vulnerable place. But faith is vulnerability. You are literally giving yourself up to something you cannot see. If that isn't vulnerable, what is?"

She asked me what I was like in church. I told her I was an observer. I wanted to participate, but had been unable to let myself go.

Once again, Smith laughed.

On some Sundays she can hardly believe that she's raising her hands and praising the Lord out loud.

"I am a control freak," she said, "but when I open my arms in front of all those people, it forces me to not be in myself and let go. When I tried to control everything, my life was not good."

Her epiphany came during a prayer when she told God that if it was time for Fred to die, she'd rely on Him. In that moment she felt a freedom that came from not being in control.

"I do believe that God talks to you and gives messages when you access Him," she said. "An empty space inside you gets filled. When I surrendered that thing I loved most—my husband—God filled me with faith.

"That is hard core," she said. "Raising your hand in church ain't nothing compared to that."

Fred recovered and built a successful consulting business. The couple wanted a family and decided to adopt, but had to remodel their house. Smith called Ms. Mary to say she wouldn't need to clean until the job was completed. But when it was time to resume the every-other-Tuesday visits, Ms. Mary had retired because of poor health.

They kept in touch with Ms. Mary, who prayed for the couple and their new daughter. Smith and her husband intended to visit Ms. Mary when the weather improved. Of course, there was always something to do and they put it off. At Easter they took family photos and sent them to Ms. Mary.

"The letter came back," Smith said. "The envelope was marked 'recipient deceased.' We were shocked. We realized that we didn't know much about Ms. Mary. We just knew she lived on the Eastern Shore of Maryland. I got online and found her obituary. She'd died of a heart attack."

Smith paused, her voice catching, not just because of emotion but also because the unborn baby—due in four months—was kicking.

"The more I think about it, she was so surreal," she said. "This seemingly random person came and changed my life. She was like a guardian angel. When I got the lesson she came to teach, she went away."

From time to time, she thinks of the stranger who led her to faith.

The prayers and Bible passages Ms. Mary handed to Smith when she was so low and all seemed hopeless are stored in a keepsake box that holds all the precious things from Smith's childhood.

She reads the prayers now and then.

One day, they will be passed on to her children.

Trust God from the bottom of your heart;
don't try to figure out everything on your own.
Listen for God's voice in everything you do, everywhere you go;
he's the one who will keep you on track.

—Proverbs 3:5–6

"When I think about what faith means to me,
it comes down to these first few lines of Proverbs 3.
The Lord shows you the way.
It's wonderful to read the Bible all the time and attempt
to understand the word of God.
But the real beauty of faith comes
when you surrender to it and let faith transform
your life from the inside out."

—Jacqui Coleman

CHAPTER 11

Morning Prayer

The sun broke through the night sky when a 1979 Buick Park Avenue wheezed into the church parking lot just after 6:00 a.m. Rust spots ate away portions of the body, the vinyl top looked like a cat had clawed it, and the crumpled front bumper dangled close to the ground. The car squealed to a stop—bad brakes—and the woman behind the wheel climbed out into the cool morning air.

She reached inside her car and changed from flip-flops into high-heeled church shoes. After uncapping a bottle of water, taking a long swig because she knew she'd be praying and singing, she grabbed her Bible.

Jacqui Coleman's family understood her need for church on Sunday, but these early-morning prayer meetings made no sense. They didn't know why she went, or what she was seeking. She'd talked about faith and the power of Jesus Christ, but they hadn't seen evidence that being faithful had made her life better.

She had been laid off—a victim of a sick economy—and was trying to keep her head above water while attending college to get a business degree. Her family figured that this God that Jacqui believed in better start working some miracles, because her unemployment checks were about to end.

Jacqui's faith never wavered, remarkable because she had no formal church foundation as a child. As a girl, Jacqui had an awareness of God, but her family didn't attend church. They had a Bible, but she never remembered reading it or thinking about God. The faith seed—what she later called it— was planted in her through the Gospel records her mother played around the house.

Her twenty-four-year-old son would have nothing to do with the church. Jacqui never pushed or preached. She had read the Bible and prayed, but only when she discovered Life Change Christian Center did she tap into God and faith, both of which smoothed out life's rough edges.

Her father had died when she was young, and she had to abandon her dream of college when she got pregnant. Two steps forward and one back seemed to be her journey. When she was fired from her first job, she sat in her car and cried, demanding to know why God let her down.

She was divorced and lived alone, not the life she'd hoped for. Faith had transformed her from the inside. She'd asked God to help her avoid using words in anger, hurting people, and pushing them away. She'd been drawn to church because being around people revealed to her how faith had softened her heart.

As she walked across the church parking lot this morning, she wasn't thinking about God or faith.

She was worried that the thirty-dollar check she'd tossed into the offering basket the previous Sunday would bounce before her unemployment check was deposited in her checking account.

Still, she smiled.

During Sunday services, my mind wandered. I'd been going to church long enough that the newness had worn off. I'd wake up not feeling religious or faithful. Watching the Dallas Cowboys on television, reading a book, or strumming my guitar was a bigger draw than church.

When I did show up, I'd think about work, an upcoming vacation, or what I needed to pick up at the grocery store on the way home. From my seat in the second-to-last row, I watched people the way I did when I was at the airport and had an hour to kill before it was time to board the plane.

More often than not, I was drawn to Jacqui, the woman I'd met long ago when she insisted I join her prayer circle. We hadn't spoken since that Sunday, and I remembered how nervous I'd been when she asked me to hold hands.

From where I sat, she made faith seem easy in the way that Tiger Woods made driving off the first tee look easy. She sang and reveled in what appeared to be pure joy—dancing, raising her hands, and saying, "Praise God." I wanted what she had—joyful faith, not something only to be studied and analyzed.

Her faith reminded me of ballroom dancing, something my wife had taken up when we joined a dance club. One of my most nerve-racking moments was when they'd call for a mixer. Men and women formed circles, and the men would be told to take two steps forward and dance with a new partner.

Dancing with my wife was okay. I could manage a fair foxtrot and waltz. But dancing with another woman—even a woman I'd grown to know quite well—was uncomfortable. I wasn't shy, but the act of dancing reminded me of all that was inadequate with my technique. My approach, even before the music started, was to apologize for being a poor dancer. By the time the song was over, I knew that most of the women agreed with my assessment.

One night, I decided to just let myself go. I didn't think about the steps or silently count in my head. I didn't apologize to my partner. I offered a strong lead, pressure in my arms, so she knew where I was guiding her. I wasn't a candidate for *Dancing with the Stars*, and my steps weren't perfect, but I had fun and looked forward to the mixers. The secret was to just dance—not think about how I looked or obsess over how uncoordinated I appeared. If I felt the music and surrendered to the moment, I could dance. What I got out of dancing depended on what I emotionally put into it.

I wanted that experience in faith.

One Sunday, when the services ended, I sought out Jacqui and asked if we could talk. Always blunt and to the point, Jacqui asked what I wanted. I reminded her of that first prayer circle and how I'd been unable to speak. I told her what I'd been doing, seeking out people who could help me understand faith. When I said I liked watching her, she took a step back and gave me a puzzled look.

No, I laughed, not like that.

Faith had always seemed so serious. Before I began attending Life Change, I'd considered church to be like the library—glances telling people to be quiet and stop being so restless. Once, when my parents took us to church as kids, my brothers and I had to split up because there wasn't enough room in the pew. My youngest brother and I kept waving to my middle brother, who was with my father near the front of the church. My mother, fed up, took us out of church and home in a cab.

I told Jacqui that she was showing me the joy of faith, and I wanted to know her secret. She frowned, excused herself from a friend who wanted a moment of her time, and pulled me to a far corner. She laid into me with what I'd later learn was part of Jacqui's charm—a no-nonsense woman who speaks her mind.

"I see you there in the back row, week after week," she said.

"You've been invited to come in, but there you stand on the outside of that door. You have to step forward and through it."

I reminded her that I had no church background to understand how to take that step, any more than I could dance a waltz without understanding how my feet were supposed to move.

Jacqui shook her head as if she were about to scold a first grader.

"Your faith foundation is different than mine or anyone else's in the world," she said. "That's the way it is in all things of life. Your background shapes you. If you grow up in the country, or the city, you're going to see things differently.

"If you come from a single-parent home or one with both parents, that will affect you," she said. "What I'm telling you is that your past has nothing to do with where you stand now on your faith journey. If you keep looking back, you'll only hold yourself back worrying about what you missed instead of looking at what is in front of you and what you will gain."

She had to go home.

"You think about what I just said," she called to me. "Then let's meet."

She'd saved me a seat at the coffee shop. When I returned with my cup, she asked me how I was doing on my faith journey. I shrugged. Honestly, I wasn't sure. I told her about some of the people I'd met and what I'd learned. What was missing was the sense of surrendering.

"What you have to understand is that faith is a relationship with the Lord," she said. "If you get nothing else out of us talking, you remember that one word: *relationship*. Faith comes, and grows, because of the time you spend with Him.

"You don't wake up one day and say I want faith, and there

it is, fully formed." You feel faith stirrings. They could come from your heart or from something you think about. Maybe it's something you read. What they are is that invitation to you to explore faith. What you do with those stirrings is up to you."

She peered at me, reminding me of a principal asking a student why he'd been acting up in class.

"You can turn away," she said. "Or you can nurture and grow that faith through prayer, meditation, and song. But you have to engage."

Why, I wondered, does the concept of faith intrigue some of us more than others, even within the same family?

"As humans we are going to believe in something," Jacqui had told me. "No one walks through this world neutral. They believe in something. Some people worship and believe in power or money. Their faith is in being called successful.

"I can't push people into the kind of faith you and I are talking about—Christian faith," she said. "All I can do is lead my life and walk my faith journey. But my faith does not make me better than my brothers and sisters. That's the key word. I am not better than anyone, in or out of the church."

She shifted in her seat and gave my forearm a gentle slap.

"Tom, you have to understand something right off," she said. "There's no one way to come to faith. There's no better way, no easy way, no hard way. There's just you and faith. What you have to do is let the love draw you in.

"Yes, if you look around that church and start asking people, you're going to find people who grew up in church families," she said. "That's no different than someone who grew up in a family that went skiing or hiking. It's part of their family history and makes them who they are. That doesn't make them better or their faith stronger."

I told her there were Sundays when I grew bored. Couldn't I stay at home, read the Bible, and pray?

"As much as faith is about you and your relationship to God, you need other people on your journey," she said. "Understand, my faith is not in the church. That said, think of faith as a fire within you. It can be a little ember. Like I said, it might be a song you hear or something you read. That little glow is faith where you are right now. The way to make the fire bigger is by throwing on more logs.

"When people come together, we learn from each other," she said. "We add to another person's faith fire. What you offer is something different from what someone else offers. You said you get something out of my singing. Praise God. Someone else, though, might not care. For them it's the prayer circle. Someone else might find their faith nurtured in a quiet conversation with someone when the church service ends.

"Not one of those people has the answer," she said. "By that I mean that the answer is not in the church as a static place, a building where people come on Sunday. Faith comes from God, but is nurtured by people. There's a reason why you've come to this church.

"Faith comes from God, but is nurtured by people."

There's a reason why you and I are talking. God wants to bring something out in you. That's one of the earliest signs of faith. It's about that relationship."

Jacqui asked if she could speak honestly to me.

"Tom, I think you're bound up a bit," she said. "You're not free."

She was right.

"Coming to faith does not mean that something is going wrong in your life," she said. "You don't have to be at rock bottom to meet Jesus. Even if things are right in your life, you know something is missing inside. You may not know exactly what it is, but somehow the satisfaction isn't there. You may have all the material things you think you need, but something is lacking. You sense there's something greater than you.

"At that moment, you're searching without knowing you are searching," she said. "When that happens, God is getting you ready for an experience. It's a heart issue, Tom. You're a soaker. It's wonderful that you like the choir and music. Praise God. But you can't just sit in your seat and soak it all in and do nothing."

One of faith's components, she told me, was giving back.

"What I'm talking about has nothing to do with tithes and what you put in the donation plate," she said. "You have to give something of yourself. What is it? I can't say. Each of us gives something differently. That's because each of us is on a different faith walk.

"Tom, God is trying to take you on a journey," she said. "Where He is taking you, I don't know. At some point—and I can't tell you when—it's going to be a heart issue for you. There will be a transformation in your heart. Right now you fight it because you don't trust. I'm not sure what you are afraid of, but you don't fully trust in God."

She banged her coffee cup hard on the table.

"What I have to say, Tom, is that you don't have faith."

When I'd asked Jacqui what specific things she did to infuse her life with faith, she told me that she made a point of attending a Tuesday-morning prayer group at church. She invited me. I always had an excuse.

I'd been reading the Bible, not from the beginning, but in Proverbs, which seemed the perfect balance to where I was on my journey: thought provoking, inspirational, and relevant to my life. I'd also started to sing when the choir asked the church to join. I wasn't belting anything out—someone standing a few feet away *might* hear me—but in my mind, it was a small victory.

My final tentative step had been an attempt to pray. In the morning, while commuting to work, I said a simple prayer based on what I got out of a series of sermons: "God, it's not about me; please remind me of that today."

Less than twelve words, but it was a start.

I no longer wanted to be what Jacqui called a "soaker." So months later, after debating whether I wanted to accept Jacqui's invitation, I set my alarm for 5:30 a.m., rolled out of bed, and set out across a city. I parked my car and opened a front door at Life Change Christian Center. From inside the sanctuary, I heard the sounds of people singing: *"Call on His name and He will answer you."*

Jacqui hadn't yet arrived, so I wandered into the sanctuary—the way I did on a Sunday—and found a seat. I felt as if I'd crashed a private party. The sanctuary held more than five hundred people. Today there were seven, each taking turns offering a prayer. The scene was too intimate, and I had no place to hide the way I did on Sundays when I sat in the second-to-last row. A minute after arriving, I felt so uncomfortable that I found a bench in an outer hallway and waited for Jacqui.

I felt relieved when her car pulled into a parking space. She walked with purpose as she made her way to the sanctuary. I followed and sat in the row behind her, eavesdropping when she bowed her head: *"Thank you, God. No matter what the circumstances, you are there, Lord."*

From across the room I heard snippets of other prayers: *"Thank you for your protection." "When we get so tired." "Comfort my family." "I'm trusting you, God."*

I heard a soft sob and saw Jacqui crying.

No pastor.

No music.

No offering.

The men and women in this room were alone and yet together. Private and yet sharing. Someone offered a prayer and others added to it: *"Thank you, God." "Comfort his family." "Hear her prayers, God."*

After about twenty minutes, I wasn't sure what to do. I felt like I was watching the dress rehearsal of a play—some great lines that had power, but not enough to be drawn into any one story.

Discreetly, making sure the mute button had been pushed, I got out my cell phone, tapped on the icon for the calculator, and started adding up my monthly bills, multiplying the amount by 12 and then dividing it by 52 to see how much I needed to save each week. I glanced at the clock: only twenty more minutes. The meeting was drawing to a close, and Jacqui walked to the front of the sanctuary, joining hands with the others to form a circle.

"Come join us."

A man motioned to me. I shook my head. I told the group—in a voice that seemed too loud—that I was there to watch. Two people in the circle dropped their hands and created a spot for me. All eyes turned toward me.

I stood.

Slowly, I made my way to the group. Jacqui took one hand; a man to my right, the other—at least my hands were not sweating. I listened to two prayers, then there was silence.

"OK," I said. "I've never prayed in public before, but I want to."

The circle murmured its approval. Jacqui told me to stand in the middle of the circle.

"Let it out," someone told me. "What are you worried about?"

And so—at 7:00 a.m. on a Tuesday morning—I prayed out loud for the first time in my life.

It rambled and stumbled. If someone had tape-recorded it, I would have been embarrassed.

But I was honest and vulnerable.

In the end, that was all that mattered.

On the way to the parking lot, Jacqui took my hand in hers.

"Tom," she said, "you're not soaking now."

Actually, I don't have a sense of needing anything personally.
I've learned by now to be quite content
whatever my circumstances.
I'm just as happy with little as with much,
with much as with little.
I've found the recipe for being happy whether full or hungry,
hands full or hands empty. Whatever I have, wherever I am,
I can make it through anything in the One
who makes me who I am.

—Philippians 4:13

"Life can be tough, but we can accomplish anything
through Christ.
We are not giving up control,
but making a conscious decision to walk with Him."

—Peter Bogren, Jr.

CHAPTER 12

Quiet Faith

The motorcycles rumbled into town about 8:00 p.m. Dirt clung to the riders' leather jackets, and their faces were burned from the summer sun and an open-road wind that, at eighty miles per hour, acts like sandpaper. Exhausted and saddle sore, they wanted a place to sleep before continuing the 2,800-mile trip, the last great adventure before one of the men had to make a decision that would alter the course of his life.

He'd been grappling with this for some time, and wondered if he was foolish. Peter Bogren, Jr., sought the advice of someone he respected and trusted—God.

Before leaving his hometown on his Harley-Davidson Fat Boy, Bogren stopped in at the small community church where his parents had taken him when he was a boy. It was in this church that he was married; it was where he and his parents came when his younger brother died in a car crash. Now at this personal crossroads, he sat in a pew, the church empty, and asked for guidance.

Bogren saw prayer as a conversation with God. A question would be posed, an answer would be given, and the process would continue for hours. He prayed this morning, but knew the answer might come somewhere out on the freeway.

He'd quit his executive-level position as vice president of

sales and marketing to return to teaching, this time to teach sixth graders. He expected the inevitable frustrations that would come from time spent in a classroom. His wife was supportive, but he knew the move would have a financial impact—a 50 percent pay cut—on the family.

This motorcycle trip with his buddies—from the Boston area to the Midwest and then back home through Canada—would be a final chance to clear his head.

Why a teacher?

Since his twenties, when he rekindled his faith after watching the birth of his son, Bogren had engaged in daily conversations with God, asking for help and guidance, and now he focused on wanting to be a teacher again to help and guide young lives.

The influence he could provide those kids was more important to Bogren than a fat paycheck and an expense account. When he'd taught and coached basketball, Bogren discovered kids asked the kind of questions—hinting at God, Jesus Christ, and faith—that adults usually avoided. He never pushed his faith, especially in school. But he didn't hide it, either. This quiet faith of his was how he lived his life.

His own faith as a teacher had been tested, as had the students who had watched their classmate lose a battle to cancer. Talking about what had happened—the *why* being the most asked question—had allowed Bogren to discover that some kids were curious about faith but feared being teased or labeled as religious nuts. Bogren believed the best thing kids could do was realize that faith wasn't confined to a church.

Bogren's faith did not come through that institution. He communicated—a word he liked better than prayer—with God throughout the day. Prayer conjured up images of someone on their knees, head bowed in a reverent moment, when what he did was talk with God.

Bogren and his buddies had found a motel not too far from the freeway. They grabbed a meal, and then Bogren went to his room to take a long shower and let his muscles relax.

Before drifting off to sleep, he prayed.

Why a teacher?

My martial arts training stressed an internal power. But Christian faith challenged me to acknowledge a power greater than myself.

I read the Bible occasionally, prayed sporadically, and continued to go to church. Over time, I found a freedom in letting go of myself and my ego and being vulnerable. I talked with an old and trusted friend in Chicago about how both of us struggled with the idea that we could control events and outcomes. Faith and prayer became a part of our conversations, which led to a refreshing sense of honesty and intimacy.

Each Sunday something connected with me: the sermon, a song, or a meeting in the parking lot where someone would pray for me to have a good week. When I discussed faith or church with my friends, I struggled not to debate them when they said they didn't believe or saw faith much differently than I did. I'd always hated pushy religious types, and I didn't want to become one.

In myself, though, I saw a bit of faith arrogance, and it reminded me of boxing. When I hit the heavy bag, jabbing, and throwing hooks, I could fool myself into believing I was a boxer. When I sparred, I'd get tagged. The pain reminded me of how much more I still had to learn.

In much the same way, I struggled in faith.

When an actress in a play my wife and I attended was from *my* church, her greatness onstage therefore reflected on me.

When Pastor Strong had to be out of town, I was disappointed in his replacement. I didn't want an understudy. At times I wanted to change parts of the church experience to fit what I wanted from it.

Occasionally, people quit coming to church. One couple left following a disagreement about church leadership. Office politics were for the outside world. Church existed to make me happy and content. Faith was supposed to be my good-luck charm.

During group prayers, before we were instructed to pray silently, someone would lead a prayer for the "good stuff"— ending hunger and stopping violence. I wasn't that noble. I once prayed that a mystery story I'd submitted to a magazine would be accepted. It wasn't.

One day I realized that I'd become addicted to the trappings of a church, which blinded me from experiencing the deep mystery that is faith.

I remembered what Pastor Red Burchfield had told me: When we equate faith with simply understanding faith, we have made faith something that we own, manage, control, and possess. It is no longer faith. It is now in our jurisdiction.

One night I picked up my guitar and started strumming. For years, I'd played guitar alone in the basement. I fooled myself into thinking that I was getting better because I could read chords and play a song. Reality hit when people at work formed a band. We had our first gig at my fortieth birthday party. I was lost, but I grew more as a musician during those three hours than I had in the years I'd played alone.

Was faith something to be done privately?

Or did faith's power, and my understanding of it, come from carrying it into the world, making mistakes, and learning as I went along?

Was stumbling—hitting the wrong chords from time to time—a part of faith?

I saw also a link between writing and faith. Bookstores are filled with books claiming to teach a person how to write—the secret is contained in the book. Even though I know it's not true, I've been searching for that book all my life.

A decade earlier, I attended a writers' conference and asked my favorite author to dinner. I wanted him to tell me how he created his stories.

Over Mexican food he listened to my questions and shrugged. He couldn't help me. Even he wasn't sure how it happened. He told me we could talk about specific tools as they related to writing, but the best advice he had for me was to write, flounder, rewrite, and do it again and again.

At this stage of my career, when I speak to writing students, they want me to reveal the secret. All I can tell them is to feel and think, to use their heads and hearts, see what others miss, and then attempt to put all that down on the page in a way that captivates others.

And so, several years into my faith journey, that is where I stood.

I believed in God and Jesus Christ.

What I sought now were teachers who could help me understand faith in a deeper way than I had once thought possible.

Peter Bogren and I began our conversation by talking about motorcycles and the relative merits of Harley—which Bogren rode—compared to my Triumph. Laughing, we agreed to disagree and made plans to get together one day for a ride on the East Coast. The motorcycle, though, was a symbolic part of my faith journey. From time to time, I'd dress down—no suit or tie—and ride my bike to church, rumbling into the parking lot and carrying my helmet inside. It was my way of showing everyone that church wasn't going to define who I was.

I told Bogren I wanted to incorporate faith in a life where the mail brings bills, the car makes funny noises, and my wife complains that I forget to clean out the cat box. Stripped down, my question was simple: How does faith move from a Sunday-only thing to play a part of daily life that might seem mundane, even ordinary?

A thoughtful man who measures his words as if he's being charged by the sentence, Bogren said nothing.

"Start with the pitfalls and roadblocks that pop up in life," he finally said. "Faith helps me remember that they're minor obstacles. Faith reminds me that God has given me great gifts to navigate life. By using those gifts and relying on faith, I'm constantly reminded that there's nothing I can't handle."

I told him I wanted to find a Christian who would be honest with me and not fall back on answers that seemed simplistic. He may be reminded that there's nothing he can't handle, but there are days when I feel overwhelmed by life. Each hour brings frustrations—traffic, looking in my wallet and finding it empty, or getting in an argument with my wife over things that are inconsequential but spark a disagreement.

"I don't want to come across as all-knowing or above it all," he said. "I get frustrated and angry and discouraged like everyone does."

Thank you, I told him.

He chuckled.

"But faith gives me this sense that God is with me," he said. "He is not going to solve all my problems—maybe not solve most of them. But He is there with me."

I told Bogren that was confusing.

How was God with him? I'd have days, even weeks, when I didn't give God a second thought. The only time I uttered the words *Jesus Christ* was when someone cut me off in traffic. I told Bogren that I'd embarked on a goal to do pull-ups, an exercise impossible to cheat at. You either pull yourself up and over the bar or you fail. I started with one and had been able to get to seven. I could easily measure my progress. Was it possible to measure my faith strength?

"There are times when I catch myself not feeling as close to God as I should," he said. "I remember that He didn't leave me."

I asked Bogren how he knew God was there. Yes, I knew the one answer: your heart beats, you breathe, and you are alive. But I wanted more than a cliché.

"Sometimes I'm communicating with God when I'm driving," he said. "Maybe at night, alone, at home. Or when I'm jogging. What you have to remember is that faith is not always spectacular. I have a very modest home, but I feel extremely blessed. I have a beautiful family. I'm thankful. Faith makes me slow down, pause, and realize what's around me.

"In addition, faith provides me with inner strength to get through the good times and the bad," he said. "Faith is an anchor in life. Two of my closest friends passed away from cancer in the last seven years.

"It was my faith that helped me as I watched them succumb to the disease and helped me make their lives a little better because I could be there for them," he said. "Faith gave me the strength I needed to not only deal with my feelings, but with their feelings."

When Bogren told me that he doesn't ask God to make life better or to do favors for him, I was ashamed to admit some of the requests I'd made.

"All I ask for is that He be there with me and give me the inner strength to deal with what I have to deal with at that time," he said. "When my brother passed away in a car crash, the natural reaction would have been for me to say 'God, please don't let this be true. Let the news be false, let it be someone else.'"

He asked, he told me, for the strength to be there for his parents.

"My best friend who passed away was a strong, robust man," he said. "At the end of his life, I'd go see him in the hospital. I'd feed him Jell-O because he couldn't lift his arms. I didn't ask Christ to take away my friend's disease. That wasn't going to happen. We all knew he was going to pass away.

"The only thing I asked for was that was his last days be made better by my being there," he said. "I counted on my faith to give me the strength to make it to that hospital every day and not get caught up in my own personal feelings and say I can't deal with this and not be there for him."

What I wanted, I told him, was a way to find faith in my daily life and to share what I believed without pressuring or preaching.

Bogren once fell away from God. But the birth of his son reminded him of his blessings, and faith once again blossomed and was deeper than ever. But he didn't want to push his beliefs. He doesn't hide his faith, but it's not something he announces. He's willing to speak about faith, especially with friends on their faith journey. At the same time, if someone says they're not comfortable with faith, or they don't believe, he doesn't force the issue.

"I have friends who don't practice any religion," he said. "I have a friend who's an atheist. He tells me that it's sad that I need to have a faith to lean on. I'm not embarrassed to talk about my faith. But I'm not one of those guys who works faith into every conversation.

"My relationship with God is very personal and something developed over a number of years," Bogren said. "For me to tell someone this is what they need to do is not right. No more than telling another married couple how they should behave in their marriage. I don't know the intricacies of their marriage, just like someone else doesn't know the intricacies of my relationship with God."

How, I asked, does a parent guide a child in faith? I wondered if I'd done the wrong thing by not insisting my children attend church, like my wife's parents had done when she was a girl. How many adults wished their parents had made them stick with piano lessons? If my parents had forced me to go to church, maybe I wouldn't be struggling now with what faith is and what role it plays in my life.

"My oldest son has a deep spirituality and a great relationship with Jesus Christ," Bogren said. "But he doesn't go to church. He doesn't believe that listening to a pastor every single week will make him a better Christian."

Bogren doesn't argue or try to convince his son to do otherwise. Everyone's relationship with Jesus Christ has to be personal, as it is with love and friendship or anything meaningful in life. If it's not personal, it's superficial. He's often closest to Christ when he's running. He literally has a conversation with Him, talking out loud about issues at work or how things are going with his family. God is always present, listening and responding, revealing Himself in ways that aren't dramatic but that remind Bogren that he's not alone in the world.

"I don't have the answers," he said. "Any person who speaks honestly about faith and God and religion will say they don't have all the answers," he said. "People who claim they know it all are off-putting and give people of faith a bad name.

"Each one of us must embark on a personal journey of faith," he said. "You can't will faith. You don't wake up one day and say from this moment on,

ᘓᕲᘓᕲ

"People who claim they know it all are off-putting and give people of faith a bad name."

I have faith. Yes, people turn to God and to faith when the chips are down and they have no hope, but the faith I'm talking about, the kind of faith that has the power to impact your life, comes from within.

"Faith doesn't always come as a lightning bolt," he said. "But you find something that locks into you. To everyone around you, it's insignificant. But to you, if you're listening and open to faith, something stirs in you. That small moment might be one thing that starts you on your journey."

The motorcycle roared to life and Peter Bogren led the way to the freeway on-ramp, two friends following each other on their bikes.

He didn't tell the waitress that morning that he hoped God would bless her with a good day. He didn't leave a Bible tract for the motel maid. He didn't tell his friends they needed to pray before breakfast.

Later, on the freeway, when the group was far from the city, Bogren saw evidence of God in the scenery, and over the rumble of the big V-twin motor, he began a conversation with God. He was open and honest, a man looking for guidance and help. Wind buffeted his body as he thanked God for his life.

Once again, he contemplated the move he was about to make.

He felt as close to God—at seventy-five miles per hour on a freeway—as he ever had in a church.

Yes, a teacher.

He rolled back on the bike's throttle and sped away, not sure what was awaiting him up the road, but ready to be there.

When we suffer for Jesus, it works out for your
healing and salvation. If we are treated well,
given a helping hand and encouraging word,
that also works to your benefit, spurring you on,
face forward, unflinching.
Your hard times are also our hard times.
When we see that you're just as willing to endure
the hard times as to enjoy the good times, we know
you're going to make it, no doubt about it.

—2 Corinthians 1:5–7

"My opportunity at a second chance
was always right in front of me.
Unfortunately, I was frozen by my own fear of 'What if?'
I was encouraged to be bold and try.
That's what opened the door for me.
I believe that God moved on my behalf
because I trusted and acted in faith.
I know that I encountered many people
who lived out this scripture in my life.
A major part of my new start is living it out in others."

—*Carl Parsons*

CHAPTER 13

Life in the Trenches

Carl Parsons quietly reached for the Bible he kept on a nightstand, slipping out of bed so as not to disturb his wife, and walked to another room. He turned on the light, settled into a chair. He turned to Proverbs, randomly selecting one to read, just like he did every morning. Once, he had been so desperate that he started his day with alcohol and painkillers. Some men have coffee throughout the day. He had needed the hard stuff to survive.

A tough guy with quick fists and a granite chin, Parsons had had his share of fights and, more often than not, came out a winner. Then he found a different power in this well-worn Bible. He concentrated now on Proverbs 15, reading slowly and thoughtfully, letting the words and message seep into his soul: *"A life frittered away disgusts God; He loves those who run straight for the finish line."*

He set the Bible in his lap, closed his eyes, and waited for inspiration, but there was none. Parsons could have been reading instructions on how to program a cell phone. He thought not of Proverbs, but of his childhood and the kid who grew up next door. Their bedroom windows were separated by 12 feet. His former neighbor now owned a home, was married, was close to his kid, and was making $70,000 a year. Parsons was trying to make amends for squandered years when he pushed everyone who mattered away.

Why, God?

He picked up the Bible again, thought about reading another Proverb, but figured it wouldn't matter. A shower and breakfast didn't clear his head. By the time he was in his car and driving to work, Parsons thought about his past and how it sometimes seemed that God wasn't being fair to him.

He had grown up in a small New Hampshire town, then bounced to Boston for a few years before hitting New York City. When he wasn't boozing and popping pills, everyone loved Carl Parsons. Problem was, Parsons always used. On to another town, leaving behind a wake of destruction, broken relationships, and regret from people who wished they'd never met the man.

Why, God?

His mother grew up in a religious home, her dad a church deacon. God the Father never made sense to Parsons, who grew up in a single-parent home and didn't know what it meant to have a father.

In time, anyone who once cared about Parsons—family and friends, an ex-girlfriend, and his daughter—wanted nothing to do with him even though he'd ended his nomadic ways and settled back in New Hampshire. He worked day labor, used, and lived in his truck in a Wal-Mart parking lot.

Finally, he had nothing left, so he sold his truck, scraped together a few bucks, and headed west to Portland to meet an old high-school friend. He had arrived by train in the heart of the city's skid road. He tracked down his friend, only to discover the guy was more addicted to drugs and alcohol than Parsons had ever been.

Years later, Parsons pulled his car onto the street and merged into traffic. About thirty minutes later, he approached a bridge—the very one he'd crossed years ago as a desperate man looking only for a warm meal. Off to his right, he saw a homeless guy holding a sign asking for money. Parsons knew the man.

Now one man was begging. The other, going to work.

Why, God?

Not a Sunday passed when I didn't hear something in church—in sermon or in song—that didn't exalt the power of Jesus Christ and God. In God's name, I was told, anything was possible. Seas were parted, the blind were made to see, and Jesus walked on water. Yet when I looked at my life, I saw no evidence of a miracle.

Yes, I was alive and my wife and children were healthy. But so, too, were friends of mine who were atheists. What was God doing for me that He wasn't also doing for them?

Yes, I could travel to the Mount Hood National Forest and be overwhelmed by the beauty, believing that it was created by God. But so could friends of mine who hadn't stepped foot in a church in years. Since I was faithful and they weren't, it made me feel as if I were paying rent on an apartment they lived in for free.

What did I get out of being faithful?

Was God like the man behind the curtain in the *Wizard of Oz*? No one saw the great and powerful Oz. In anonymity, people granted him powers that he didn't possess. The "gifts" he gave to the Tin Man, the Lion, and the Scarecrow—a heart, courage, and a brain—were attributes within themselves. Was the God I worshipped any different from the Wizard of Oz?

The Bible was full of miracles—all conveniently in the distant past—but they had no relevance to my life. I wanted God to do something for me, something specific that I could use to prove His existence. Walking to work each morning I'd pass homeless people in doorways. At a coffee shop I became friends with a mentally challenged woman who told me street punks stole her purse.

Where was God?

When the lottery payout reached $200 million, I put $5 in the machine for a ticket. I prayed for a winner, promising God I'd give half to Life Change Christian. I didn't even match one number. The challenge, obviously, was absurd, but He had His chance. I looked for instances where God made a difference. I sought not examples of contemplation or comfort—things a close friend could provide—but moments where a great power revealed itself.

"The questions you ask are universal," said Marty Guise, a man I met in the Midwest. "It boils down to this: How do you—I, and all of us—deal with what we perceive to be inequity in the world? I'm not speaking of great injustices in lands far away. I'm talking about the things in your life, my life. The best way to phrase it might be this way: some things stink."

Guise, a man of deep faith, told me that one of his biggest struggles has been dealing with his son's Tourette's syndrome, a condition that causes a person to undergo involuntary tics of the body. Although his son is better, there was a time when he couldn't control himself. He'd need an aide in school because he'd fall into a daze and wander away. Intellectually, Guise understood the concept that sin entered our world and the ramifications are disease, illness, and death. But what, dear God, did a little boy do to deserve this?

That question served as a wave, crashing day after day on his faith and eroding it over time. And then friends adopted a girl who later had juvenile rheumatoid arthritis. I told Guise that to use the word *sin* in any case involving a child seemed appalling and almost pushed me away from the idea of a God. This perspective made God seem like an abusive spouse who beats his wife, making her believe she's done something wrong and that she needs to earn her way back into his good graces.

"Faith is about wrestling with questions, doubts, and emotions," he told me. "When you feel yourself wrestling, that's a good thing because you're engaged."

At one point, Guise told me, he was so mad at God that he no longer saw the purpose of faith.

"I had a morning where I was crying and raging out to God," he said. "Some people claim to hear voices all the time. I'm not one of those people. But I heard a voice in my head that said "I have a son, too." It was this gentle whisper. It knocked me over. I was blown away, and a thousand thoughts hit me in a millisecond. God knows my pain because Jesus Christ was born to die."

I had to be blunt: So what?

"If God is a loving God," he asked, "how do you put life's difficulties in that same construct of faith and understanding God, and wanting to believe in Him? I certainly had those battles. What faith holds for us is that Jesus experienced life. His friends betrayed Him. He was rejected and challenged. What that means is that we have a Savior who knows us and knows what it's like to live like us. He really did walk the path that we are walking and experience the things we experience. He never dealt with a computer crash, but He struggled with the emotional investment in people and saw them walk away from Him.

"Our faith can become routine until it's challenged with pain or struggle," he said. "There's pain in the world. You cannot avoid it. If we didn't know pain, we would not know love. If we hadn't experienced difficulty, we wouldn't know the blessing of triumph. Pain helps us grow. That may sound like a pat answer, but it's the truth. Feeling the pain helps us understand the love."

That's great for Guise. But what about his son? Where is God for him? Why does God punish the most innocent among us?

These were all questions, Guise told me, that he wrestles with. He told me about the day a couple of kids at school teased his son because of his tics. That night, his son—crying—asked his father why. His father's answer—one that never varies—was "I don't know."

"We pray as a family every night at dinner," Guise told me. "My prayer is to help us reflect Christ more. If we can do that, then it will be better for my son, for the people around him, and for the world. It may sound crazy, but the challenge is for us to become more like Christ. If my son is more like Christ, his ability to deal with his Tourette's will be that much greater."

What stayed with me long after Guise and I parted ways was that Guise hadn't prayed for God to take away the Tourette's. Just as Bogren had done, this father prayed for the strength to deal with life where he now stood.

It made me think about what had stirred in me when I first attended Life Change. I wasn't looking for a miracle—a winning lottery ticket, a new car, or a paid-off mortgage—but a force to change me and who I was.

Perhaps, I now realized, I was defining a miracle in the wrong way and looking in the wrong places.

That's when I met Carl.

The early-morning drunks and bums shuffled to life, as commuters—rushing to get to their offices—passed by me on the busy street where I waited for Carl Parsons. He stepped out of the Union Gospel Mission and shook my hand, but before we could speak, a drunk staggered up to Parsons to ask if he knew where he could get something warm. A rainstorm had passed through the city and the man's sweater—too big and with many holes—looked like a sponge with water dripping from the sleeves. Parsons returned to the mission, found a blanket, and handed it to the man, who took it without uttering a word of thanks.

"When you're ready," Parsons told the man, "you come see me. I'll give you some water and a sandwich."

The man said nothing as he weaved down the street.

"I can't fix that man's life," Parsons said. "But in this moment, right here on this sidewalk, I am God's ambassador."

He stood there until the man disappeared around the corner.

"I was that man," Parsons said. "I see myself in every one of the faces of the people out here."

He pointed to the mission door and led the way inside.

"I'm one of God's miracles," he said while we waited for the elevator.

After landing in Portland, Parsons burned through his money and rented a room in a fleabag of a motel. One morning, hungry and broke, he walked across a bridge and stood in line with more than a hundred people waiting for a free sack lunch at the mission.

In line Parsons met a man who told him about a mission program called Life Change. Parsons took his lunch, walked back to his motel, and wondered where he'd go next. He was lying on the bed when he remembered what the man had told him. He rolled out of bed, slung his backpack over his shoulder, and walked back across the bridge. He asked someone at the main desk about the program and was told it was a four-year commitment. Other than booze and pills, Parsons was commit-

∽∾

Other than booze and pills, Parsons was committed to nothing. But he figured he could scam a few meals and be on his way.

ted to nothing. But he figured he could scam a few meals and be on his way. He tucked his backpack behind a Dumpster down the block so he could retrieve it when he took off, just the way he always had.

"That was six years ago," Parsons told me. "What kept me here and what saved me was faith."

"Was it God?" I asked. "Or did you finally decide you had nothing left in life?"

"God," Parsons said quickly. "Let me explain what I mean about faith and how you can't separate God from people. Faith was when I was looking at thirty-five people who had done this program before me. I was literally looking at guys who had lived here three or four years. They'd put families back together. They'd seen children again. They got jobs and were going to work. They were sober every day. The faith carrot was if that guy could do it, then I could too."

Even with the best of intentions, the old Carl reemerged. He broke a few rules and should have been kicked out of the program. Mission officials gave him a second chance with the provision that he think about what he'd done and what he was risking. They told him they believed in Carl Parsons.

"I figured if they had faith in me, then I could take a chance on myself," he said. "For the first time in my life, I was going to trust someone other than myself—God. My first bunkmate had been in the program a year. He left six months after I came here, and not ninety days later, drank himself to death. That showed me that faith is something you train in. You start with a small amount. You grow it and take care of faith. You let God enter your life.

"Everyone experiences a unique moment where God calls his or her name," he said. "It's not a big booming voice out of the dark. It's a moment when God says, 'It's time; put up or shut up.' I put up."

Believing in a good and gracious God was difficult. A man who lives by his wits never lets anyone in his heart. To survive, Parsons had to fight every instinct. He had to believe and trust in something unseen. Over a period of months and years, he moved faith from something outside of himself—the prayer groups, Bible passages, and mission meetings—to something inside.

"Going through it was tough," he said. "If you've ever been to the gym, you'll understand. That first day you lift weights and it hurts. The next time it's a little better. Six months later it feels so good that you can't imagine a time when you didn't lift.

"It burned the first few times I had to do something in faith," he said. "But I saw there were things I accomplished beyond my abilities and desire because of my faith in God."

I told Parsons about my work with pull-ups, moving from just one to seven. My goal was to do fifteen. Did faith have similar steps?

"When someone has spent the better part of twenty years drinking every day, there's a faith moment when he puts the bottle down and doesn't pick it up for an hour," Parsons said. "And then for a day. There's a faith moment when you're in the bathroom throwing up and wishing you were dead, but you hang in there because you pray to God and hang on, believing He is with you at that very low moment.

"The only contentment I found was when I stopped and said that is not my life," he said. "It is God's life, and I will do what He asks me to do. I had no idea what that meant, or where He would take me. I had no idea if I'd like it or if I could succeed. But I truly believed that God was invested in me."

I asked Parsons how we know what God wants us to do with our lives. If I were an alcoholic, it would be clear: quit drinking. But what about when the problems aren't as simple as a fifth of Jack Daniels?

"There's a peace that comes over you when you tell God you're lost and afraid," Parsons said. "We fight that vulnerability. But taking that step pulls you away from yourself. In that way, you get what you need. You don't get an answer. But many times what we seek is not an answer but understanding. At the end of the day, it's a faith step. I would love to tell you that the faith journey gets easier as time goes on. But I don't think it does.

"Every time I think I've conquered faith, life circumstances put a faith step in front of me that's just a little bit farther than I'm comfortable with," he said. "It's like crossing a river on rocks. Just when you think you're in stride, the rocks get just a little farther apart.

"I'm like most people in that life is most dangerous when I'm in my comfort zone," he said. "When I know where the next rock is and I'm bouncing along, I stop paying attention. I stop seeing the obstacles closing in and the danger looming. A God who loves me sees me in my comfort zone and says that before I fall and break my leg, He's going to make me work a little harder for this one. In the moment, I resent it. I think I have faith down, and then something happens and I feel a bit lost again. But every time I stretch my stride and hit those rocks, the reward is so much better."

I walked to a mission window and pointed at a skyscraper across the street, home to law firms and big business. I asked Parsons if he thought the faith journey was different for the men and women who worked there.

"There's a parable where the rich man comes to Jesus, and

Jesus says, if you love me, lay down all you have and follow after me," he said. "The rich man says that's too much. Jesus says if you can't do that, then you are not worthy.

"Do I think there are rich people who follow after God with all their heart?" Parsons asked. "Absolutely. But I think it's a lot more difficult for them than it is for someone who is down in the gutter. The rich person has an out from faith. He's got things, the trappings that he can use to hide from the world and himself. A man in the gutter has nothing. People know who he is and what he is. He knows who he is and what he is.

"Faith is played out down in the trenches of life," he said. "That's where all of us, one way or the other, live. There seems to be nowhere to turn. All the stuff that used to work is worthless. Right then, you have to decide. For me, the answer comes back to faith. Lead me, God."

If God is loving and all-powerful, why doesn't He create hundreds of miracles for all those men and women in the gutter?

"Faith is available to a lot of people, but they choose not to accept it," Parsons said. "The very first faith step is to admit that you don't have all the answers. So many people, and I was one of them, think they do. It's scary to say the three words *I don't know.* Those words lead you to your first step on the faith journey.

"When you make that first attempt, you admit that you are broken or flawed or that you have troubles," he said. "You admit that you aren't perfect. How many people hide because they know—deep inside—they aren't perfect and don't want people to judge them? The circle closes in when you do that."

At that moment, Parsons told me, the Holy Spirit comes into a life.

"You have a choice," he said. "What are you going to do?

At that point, if you make the right choice, you're suddenly aware that you're not alone. You have hope. It may be a glimmer off in the distance, but for the first time you see a way out, or back as the case may be.

"Life is lived on a flat plain," he said. "I'm either headed toward God or away from God. There's no other choice. Do I stumble? Sure. But I keep walking toward God. Faith is the magnetic north of my moral compass that helps me follow the path with all its twists and turns. A life without faith always leads away from God. When I get off course, and who doesn't, I use faith to turn me back in the right direction."

Parsons said he runs into men on the street who want nothing to do with God or Jesus Christ because they fear it makes them look weak. Too many men see faith as something for guys who wear loose-fitting linen pants, play guitar, and have long, flowing hair. That image makes faith seem effeminate.

"I had to change my opinion of what Christ looks like in order to embrace faith," he said. "Take a look at the classic Anglo-Saxon picture of Jesus. He has a dress on, long wavy hair, and blue eyes. His beard is primped and he's holding flowers. Come on. That's not me. That's not a lot of guys. All that does is make God look as if He's living in a cloud where He plays with angels and cherubs."

That perception of Christ—a pacifist hippie who talks about turning the other cheek—was tough for Parsons to overcome. But as he read more about Christ's life, Parsons realized how much he and Christ had in common. Christ was no weakling. He was a carpenter. During his day-laborer job, Parsons had spent time with men like that. They had calluses on their hands, their forearms are 8 inches around. Call one of them weak and flowery at your own risk.

I told Parsons that he reminded me of some of the Hells

Angels I'd come to know over the years. They could be exceedingly polite. Over beers I once told a group of them—after they were comfortable with me, of course—that they were easygoing. They laughed and told me, don't ever mistake kindness for weakness. I saw that up close when three men the size of pro football players decided—in the middle of an upscale restaurant—to act like tough guys and hit a Hells Angel.

Parsons laughed and said that Jesus Christ—not the guy depicted in Sunday school paintings—was a tough guy, too. He was an outdoorsman, tended sheep, and knew how to survive while surrounded by enemies. That epiphany—that Christ was not a sissy—drew Parsons deeper into faith.

"A lot of my friends are big guys," he said, "but we hold hands and pray together. What that shows is that you don't have to be phony, pretentious, or soft to love God. You can be a man, go to work, drive a dump truck, and still have faith."

I peered out a mission window where I could see the homeless, the drunks, and the addicts. During the next few months, men and women on that sidewalk would die, shoot dope again, or start the morning with a quart of beer. With all his power, why couldn't God change those lives and save everyone such pain?

"He could, but would it benefit them?" Parsons asked. "Isn't the striving in life better than just floating along? Life is going after it, pursuing it. Faith is no different. You want it? Pursue it. I'm stepping out and I may fall. But I'm going forward with faith. It doesn't guarantee success. In fact, you're going to experience a lot of hurts and failures. But you get up and try again the next day."

Carl Parsons worked through lunch and made sure he was caught up before leaving early. On the way to his car, he turned to look back at the mission and realized how far he'd come from the day he stood in line for a free lunch: he was married, his bills were up to date, and he was in the process of restoring a relationship with his daughter.

He left downtown and, fifteen minutes later, turned into a hospital parking lot. He didn't need to check with the woman at the front desk. The floor nurses and the supervisor at the nurses' station waved to him as he pushed open the door to his friend's room.

From the bed, his friend smiled at Parsons.

The big man with a workingman's hands tenderly took the small man's hand in his own. He bowed his head and in a soft but sure voice offered a prayer.

Three men had once been roommates at the mission.

One was now a drunk and begging for money near a bridge.

The other worked at the mission, read Proverbs each day, and tried to live a life that showed God works miracles.

The third man, at twenty-six, was dying.

Six months earlier he'd gone to the doctor because he wasn't feeling well. Tests and exploratory surgery revealed a body full of tumors. He had about a month.

When Parsons had been depressed, overwhelmed, unsure whether he could stay straight, and wondering almost hourly if there was a God, the dying man in the bed had been there for him, his faith unwavering.

Now it was Parsons' turn to show that same kind of faith. Unspoken was the question that had haunted Parsons weeks earlier.

Why, God?

They talked about Jesus Christ, of God, of love, and of hope.

A life, Parsons told his friend, is lived to reveal a purpose beyond the here and now.

His friend agreed.

He offered his own prayer.

If anyone had passed by the room, they would have seen two men holding hands.

" 'And when did we ever see you sick or in prison
and come to you?'
Then the King will say, 'I'm telling you the solemn truth:
Whenever you did one of these things to someone
overlooked or ignored, that was me—you did it to me.' "

—Matthew 25:40

"This verse is talking about seeing God in every person and
recognizing that God's spirit is within each person equally.
It talks about being compassionate and caring for others,
because what you do to others—even the least among us—
we are actually doing to God. Because, God is their essence."

—*Lt. Dan Willis*

CHAPTER 14

Good and Evil

Dan Willis picked up his office telephone and listened, nodding from time to time and quietly comparing notes with another cop who wanted to talk about the previous day's funeral. One of their own had been murdered in her own home. Across Southern California, cops were trying to make sense of the tragedy.

After hanging up, Willis listened to the police radio in his office—the dispatcher sending cops from one call to another—and thought about his own career. In the police academy, instructors had emphasized that a cop's career is built on a foundation of evidence and precision. Is that handgun a revolver or a semiautomatic? How far—in feet and inches—was the body from the front door? What about DNA? If you can't prove it, instructors said, you don't have a case.

As he sat at his desk, Willis wondered what evidence he had when it came to the question of God.

His father had left religion to his wife, who took Willis and his brothers to church. At night she'd read to them, often choosing biographies of famous people who'd lived spiritual and faithful lives. His mother said that a life is a gift that belongs to God and that should serve and honor God.

Unlike his brothers, who drifted from church, Willis never

left. In his junior year in high school, he decided to serve God by becoming a cop. He did a stint as a reserve officer and, after graduating from college, landed a full-time position at the La Mesa Police Department near San Diego.

His faith had been tested throughout his career, but this week had been brutal. After all that had happened, Willis knew that a defense attorney would ask the jury how they could believe in this alleged God when the evidence clearly showed He didn't exist.

The week began when a man walking home from the store was confronted by a group of men in a car. After pulling over and stealing the beer he'd just purchased, they beat and kicked him for the fun of it. The victim, in the hospital with a severe brain injury, could die. Police had no suspect or clues, and Willis knew there was little chance the assailants would be caught.

Days later, Willis attended an autopsy for an eighteen-month-old baby. X-rays showed multiple breaks and bruises, indicating he'd been beaten during most of his short life.

Yesterday Willis had attended the funeral for a detective from another jurisdiction. The woman, about to retire after a thirty-one-year career as a sex crimes detective, had prevented thousands of children from being abused by arresting offenders and sending them to prison.

She'd been stabbed to death.

By her stepson.

Who also killed her daughter.

What kind of God would allow this to happen?

Three days after church, I walked to the police station and took the elevator to the detective division to meet a sergeant who wanted to tell me about the most unusual case in his career. He pulled out a file and told me the basics: an unsolved murder and a pastor who was headed to prison for twenty years.

In the early 1990, an eighteen-year-old man and his twelve-year-old foster brother were leaving a convenience store when a young wife and mother of two pulled into the parking lot. The man thought she was cute and also noticed, when she bought a few items, that she had money. He hung around the store, flirted with her, and then asked if she wanted to meet around the corner to smoke some dope.

She agreed and followed his car in hers. They pulled to the curb. He walked to her car. Leery, she told him to leave. He put a small-caliber handgun to the side of her head and pulled the trigger. He took $60.

Decades later, detectives received a tip and began a long investigation, tracking down the foster brother, by then in prison. They squeezed him and he gave up the name of his partner, a man who'd eventually changed his life. He'd given up drugs and crime. He'd married, had a child, and was a pastor.

When confronted, he confessed. His wife and kids had no idea of the secret from his past. He'd struggled with what he'd done, talked with a counselor, but kept quiet because he didn't want to hurt his family. He attended church and taught others about God. On the day he was sentenced to prison, the man agreed to help the victim's family heal by meeting with them to answer questions. He accepted responsibility for what he'd done and planned to pastor in prison.

Years earlier, when I wasn't going to church, it would have been a fascinating story. Now, it was more than that. Where was God, and what was His role in the crime and aftermath?

The same questions troubled me a month earlier when I'd covered the sentencing of a man who'd pled guilty to the most horrific rape case the prosecutor had seen in fourteen years. I arrived about twenty minutes early and found a seat in the third row, next to a woman and her daughter, who looked to be about three. The defendant, led into the courtroom by guards, was being sentenced to twenty years in prison. A year earlier his fiancée's daughter had come to the hospital complaining of cramps. Doctors discovered she was thirty-one weeks pregnant.

She was ten years old.

A plea deal was arranged to spare the girl the trauma of a trial. Her mother walked to a microphone to tell the judge that the man had stolen her daughter's innocence. She'd never hurt anyone. The girl gave birth via a cesarean, had a scar on her stomach, and was undergoing counseling.

When the guards helped him out of his seat, the defendant turned and nodded to the woman sitting next to me. She was his new girlfriend, there with her daughter. Before guards led the man out of the courtroom, he whispered to them, "I love you." On the other side of the courtroom, the victim's mother screamed: "I hope you burn in hell!"

Would this woman get her wish?

Would the man end up in hell?

Or was twenty years in prison—where inmates hated child abusers—going to be his hell?

And—once again—where was God?

The police department lobby looked like every cop station I've been inside: Spartan, chairs that couldn't be damaged by troublemakers, and a receptionist sitting behind bulletproof class.

Willis appeared from a side door and said nothing as we walked up the steps from the lobby to his second-floor office. He pointed to a chair on the other side of his desk. Years of writing about cops taught me that even when releasing the most basic information, they're rarely open around reporters, fearing their word will be twisted by people who have little understanding of the realities of their world.

I wanted to explore who he was as a man and a cop. He told me he was a kid who liked church because faith gave his life direction; as he grew older, faith allowed him to view life as more than a series of unconnected events.

"Faith starts with a belief that our spirit is the essence of us," he said. "We have a mind and we have a body. We also have spirit that controls the other two. The spirit is who we really are. All the other things—church, the sermons, the Bible, and prayer—connect with that spirit. We're basically spiritual beings having a human experience. That means that all of life is an expression of God."

I saw an opening for my first hard question for him, but let him continue. God, he said, is here to give His blessing and help to everyone. But humans put up obstacles. Some people, like his brothers, feel they're better off in control. Others don't believe. Faith, though, makes life more interesting, exciting, and fulfilling, each day being an adventure with God. The inherent nature of faith is that it comes to each person differently, or sometimes, not at all. Faith must be cultivated. Only through nurture and practice does faith have a place in our lives. Claiming faith isn't enough.

"Faith takes time," he said. "Giving up control is a struggle. The more we give up our life, the more we realize that we're temporary caretakers of our body, and the more we give ourselves to God. The less important our selfish interests become. What I do to someone else, I see as doing to God."

A police officer sees the terrible things we do to each other. I'm not talking about accidents or illness, but where one human does something that a loving God shouldn't allow.

"I realize the existence of evil," he said simply. "I know a lot of people don't like to talk about evil. There is another force at work other than God. It's not nearly as powerful, but it's a force that can influence people to do these cruel, violent, and evil things."

I told Willis I'd been in the presence of evil before.

Once in a man I interviewed in prison. He hired someone to kill his wife while she was on a business trip, staging the crime to make it look like a robbery. The man was a psychopath. He had the ability to study someone, determine what was lacking in his or her life—love, acceptance, power—and become the person to fill that hole. That was a certain kind of evil. So, too, the hit man I met in Los Angeles. At first glance he was mild mannered, standing about 5 feet 7 and not strong or tough, the kind of man, I thought that evening, that someone might yell at during a moment of road rage. But his eyes, cold and unfeeling, were frightening. I'd seen eyes like that only one other time in my life.

From a distance, he looked like any six-year-old boy: dark hair, laughing and playing with other kids. When I sat down with him, I saw in his eyes something that chilled me. My instinct—an almost animal-like feeling within me—told me this was evil. His counselor told me I was right. Even with treatment, this boy would likely be a criminal, and he wouldn't be surprised if, even with years of help, the boy became a predator and one day killed someone.

The boy had been sexually and physically abused by both parents from birth. At one point, they tossed him into a garbage can. Authorities finally rescued him and made him a ward of the state. When I met him, he was living at a long-term counseling center where Oregon's toughest cases—the kids who had failed other programs—landed.

What, I asked Willis, is evil, and where is God?

Why didn't God protect the woman on her business trip?

The little boy was clearly a victim. Why had God allowed evil to destroy his life? In time, though, he'd be the one destroying other lives.

God seemed content to sit on the sidelines.

Willis had no answers, at least none that would satisfy me, he said. He, too, had spent a career asking the same questions. But as bleak as his world can so often seem, he said he manages to find hope.

"People aren't possessed by evil," he said. "But they are spiritually sleepwalking and unable to evolve into what God wants them to be. It's apparent to me that life is spiritually evolving. Go back a thousand years, and the cruelty and barbarity of the world was unbearable. There has been progress."

He saw on my face that I wasn't buying his answer.

"No one can pretend to know the mind of God," he said. "I don't know all the answers."

He fell silent for a moment, and I knew that he was thinking of some of the crimes he'd investigated.

"The greatest gift God has given us is free choice," he said. "Without that we'd be robots. With that choice we can do incredibly good things or incredibly bad things."

He leaned back in his chair.

"In this job," he said, "I've seen both. My faith is a buffer between my life and my work. Given where I work, people might think that it would be impossible to logically believe in God. My faith helps me process and attempt to understand some of the bad things I deal with day in and day out."

Willis sat silently, maybe for thirty seconds, before speaking again.

"I think cops with faith have more tools to draw upon to help them," he said. "It helps me sustain an inner spirit. This job can drain the life out of you and destroy normal relationships at home. Without my faith, I would not survive this job.

I've known cops with no faith who lose hope or perspective. They drink too much. Their mind, body, and spirit can't process what they see."

He then turned to what would happen to the rapist and to all the criminals who hurt innocent people. He said God holds people accountable for their actions, but he does not believe in a hell. That would mean, he said, that evil is more powerful than God.

"Evil has to serve God's purpose, or why would He allow it?" Willis said. "Who is to say what God, in His ultimate wisdom, decides? What I try to do is bring some peace and order to society.

"The concept has to go beyond the question of why a good person died and a dirtbag lived," he said. "The essence of my life, your life, even the life of the doper I arrested just the other day is what makes us alive. That is God."

I was surprised to hear Willis say that guilt should not be a part of faith, that God is forgiving and we need to forgive ourselves. That doesn't mean, he said, that we can hurt or kill and with God's help wipe the slate clean.

"There's justice here, and justice later," Willis said. "What God cares about is our effort. As long as we're trying, he's there to pick us up and help us heal."

Willis said he considers himself in partnership with God—he's doing God's work to protect people from evil.

"The only way to keep evil people from harming others and causing so much suffering in this world is for good people to stand up to it and try to fight it," he said. "You are still, of course, going to have suffering and hard times and trials. Part of what I've come to learn over the years is that hard times are for our own good. When we suffer, it's God's way of getting our attention and getting us to refocus on what is important in life."

I'd been to Parents of Murdered Children meetings. I'd listened to people in those rooms speak of crippling pain. I heard nothing that would indicate they were thankful for what they had been through.

"Yes, my faith is shaken when I see such horrific things," he admitted. "Just when you think you've seen about the worst people can do to each other, you come into work and another case comes in."

All he can do, he told me, is to continue believing in God and fighting evil. That's why he became a cop.

"I worked a case where a man was taken 115 miles away from here," he said. "He was killed and his head and hands were cut off. We never found body parts. There was no witness, confession, known murder scene, DNA, or other physical evidence. Not even a cause of death. But the investigators and I were able to get two brothers convicted for first-degree murder six years after the crime.

"That's fighting evil," he said. "I had a case where a man killed his girlfriend. We've never found her body, but we were able to convict him seven years after the murder. That's fighting evil.

"A man came in at age twenty-eight and reported being molested when he was eight," he said. "We worked that case, got a search warrant, and found several pictures that the molester took of that kid. He'd blown them up and framed them, photos of a kid posing naked. They were his most prized possession. We got that guy convicted twenty-seven years after the crime.

"That's the stuff that renews my faith, as God works through us to restore justice and to prevent further harm to others," he said. "To bring some sense of justice to victims and to the families."

Most of us, I told him, don't get an opportunity to serve or know God in the middle of a war. We're trying to get through the day and find a bit of meaning and hope in our lives. None of us, including myself, is particularly heroic.

"My feeling is that everyone can significantly serve God no matter what they do for a living or where they are in life," he said. "You do that by living a faith-filled life as best as you are able.

"No one says you have to be a hero," he said. "The world doesn't need more heroes. What the world does need is good, compassionate people of faith living meaningful lives and taking good care of their children, families, friends, strangers in need, and the community. What you can do is become an example to people."

"Faith is not just going out and talking about your faith," he said. "Faith is living a good life the best you are able. There might be one or two people in this department who know that I'm a person of faith. But I know that people come to me and trust me because of how I try and display my character.

"In every situation—your conversations with people, with customers if you are a salesperson, or any situation—you can tap into faith," he said. "Faith is seeing God's life in people and relating to the presence of God in that person. Faith and God are always available, but it's our responsibility to tap into them. Electrical outlets are scattered all over this room. Electricity is everywhere. But it doesn't do me any good unless I tap into the plug to access it."

Willis has had cases where he felt led to talk to a particular person or to look for evidence in a certain area. He believes God is guiding him.

"That's what people of faith can do in any job or situation," he said. "To give ourselves to God in order to be used for good and to bless others. People who have not experienced faith see it as a weakness. Having faith is courageous. I know that I'm a small, insignificant person. But within me, within every one of us, is the potential to do very good things. How? Get out of the way and allow yourself to be used and led by a higher power."

I looked around his office and asked him if he saw himself as a cop or a man of God.

"I see myself always as a man of God," he said. "Being a police officer is not who I am but what I do for God. I say a prayer every day asking that I be used by God to be at the place where I can be most useful. I ask that God give me the right thing to say at the right moment. I ask that God allow me to do something good and useful to serve Him. No matter what you are doing, if you do it with an attitude of serving God and wanting to do good in communion with this higher power and source of what I see as all life, then it makes everything meaningful."

He made me think about a recent case I'd written about. One of Oregon's oldest unsolved murders involved a six-year-old girl who walked to the store one day in the 1960s and never came home. They found her body along a remote road. She'd been raped and murdered. The girl's mother, who had once been an active church member and sang in the choir, told me she refused to step in a church for decades because she believed God had abandoned her and her daughter.

Although the killer was never caught, the mother had a sense of closure when a detective who had reopened the case drove more than five hours to see her, bringing with him the girl's clothes, the case reports, and an answer to who he believed killed the girl. I sat at the kitchen table that afternoon and watched how the detective's compassion made a difference in this woman's life.

"Faith is so personal and private," Willis said. "I can't start talking like you and I are now with someone who has suffered a loss. Who knows what their belief system or background is? The best I can hope for is to listen, be compassionate, and to find a kind word or two that can give some hope. I tell them that if there's a way I can bring the person to justice who did this to them or their family members, I will do what I can. It's tough when you see the suffering that people are going through. It's hard to suffer with them.

∞∞

"God does not do things to harm people. People do things to themselves, or to others."

"That's how officers lose some of themselves," he said. "An officer gets numb. Faith helps me navigate my world. God does not do things to harm people. People do things to themselves, or to others.

"I might not understand it," he said. "I don't have to have the answer. I have reverence and trust in God, thinking that there is some purpose, reason. Bad things happen. But faith gives me hope. If I was on my own, if I had no faith, I'd be a basket case."

How about helping fellow officers?

"I've not talked this openly to officers about faith," he said. "A few close friends know how I feel. What I've done recently is approach the chief. I told him we train officers to be physically safe. We teach them how to be fit and we teach them about the law. We train their bodies and minds. But we do nothing to nurture their spirits, that part of them that makes them want to be police officers, to serve others, and do good. I asked the chief if I had permission to form a spiritual-emotional wellness committee. The purpose would be to teach officers how to process the pain and evil that we see day in and day out and how to remain emotionally and spiritually well.

"It's not a religious thing," he said. "But when you talk to someone, you can't deny there's something beyond a mind and a body. What do you call that? It is your spirit; it's what makes us human. That's where faith comes into play. How I keep my faith in this job is to think about how God can allow me to affect officers' lives."

I've written about cops who joined the force, so full of a desire to do good and change the world. And I've written about their retirement, too, when they're jaded and think only about their pension benefits. How is it possible for any cop to maintain a sense of hope when day after day they deal with nothing but bad news?

"I tell cops that when they catch someone and send them to prison, they need to think of all the people who will not be victimized because of their good work," he said. "Unknown people will not be raped or robbed or have a family member brutalized or murdered.

"So many people will be saved from harm, even though they will never know it and will never be able to thank you," he said. "I use this as a motivator to keep officers connected to the purpose of our work protecting others. People might not think there is a faith and spiritual component to law enforcement. There is. Protecting others is an aspect of God."

Willis said it is never as easy as he made it sound. He can feel so connected to God, and then a crime takes place that challenges his beliefs.

"I have to actively keep renewing and accessing faith," he said. "I must actively keep seeking God for comfort, guidance, peace, and understanding. I've found that everyone's faith is challenged. Something will happen to throw us off, then God taps us on the shoulder by some experience and we again feel connected to Him. Our lives are a journey. Nothing is consistent. Nothing stays always good or always bad.

"There are times when we might even doubt the existence of God," Willis said. "But He is there, in every moment waiting for us. For me, faith is being in command of this tremendous power that can potentially change or improve any situation in life."

He could get a call in the next hour, I said, that would challenge everything he just told me.

"That's my world," he said. "I can't answer some of your questions, maybe many of your questions. My answers might not make sense to you. You might think I'm rationalizing faith. In some ways, what I do and the world I work in makes my faith stronger than someone who only goes to church on Sunday and listens to hymns and a good sermon before they head home."

He pointed to the lobby and said that he has often been called to come downstairs to meet someone who wants to speak with him.

"I can arrest the same people over and over again, put them in jail only to see them out on the street again," he said. "And I ask what am I doing here? Then this man came in and asked for me. I didn't remember him. He said I arrested him a year ago and he's cleaned up. I said I was proud of him. He told me that arrest was a turning point in his life and he wanted to thank me. He's not the only one. I remember what I'm here for. The first time that happened, I saw value in what I do for God.

"I've come to understand that when I'm arresting people, they don't like me at the moment and may even want to kill me," he said. "But their soul needs my help. My prayer is that I may be providing the negative consequence to their criminal and destructive behavior that could be the catalyst to cause them to change."

Willis told me that eight years ago he heard about something called "bum fights." Homeless men were given enough booze to get drunk and then encouraged to fight. The winner got more beer. The fights were filmed and distributed on the Internet. Willis saw the men as victims.

"It was one of hardest investigations I ever worked on, but four men were eventually convicted," he said. "The bottom line is that one of the homeless men had been a chronic drunk since he was twelve. He was in his late forties when bum fights started. After we got the organizers arrested and prosecuted, a citizen came forward and took this homeless guy under his wing.

"The homeless man has been clean and sober now for eight years. He's going to college campuses talking about homeless issues and alcoholism. He's been to the State Capitol talking with legislators. That's what renews my faith and hope in God. Here is someone who for over thirty years was a chronic, homeless drunk who officers would pick up out of the gutter all the time. This rotten, stinking bum who so many thought was merely a useless drunk and did nothing but cause problems.

"We found him being victimized and, I believe with God's influence, did something about it," he said. "God not only used others to save his life, but is now using him to teach others about the plight of the homeless and alcoholism in order to create more change.

"Remember how I said that God taps us on the shoulder?" he asked. "My constant prayer is that God use me to be that tap on someone's shoulder."

I asked Willis what I needed to learn from him. He said, some days even the strongest of believers question God's existence. In his job, that question can arise with every call and crime scene. But a man in an office or a mother in a quiet home faces the same question. Something spiritually will challenge all of us and knock us down.

For him it could be the murder of a fellow cop, a baby's brutal death after a life of torture, of having to investigate a case of a truly innocent victim. For others it could be not getting the job promotion, a child estranged from a parent, or a marriage on the brink.

"That moment—and how we handle it—is when we can rediscover God," he said. "We want to run from the problem, blame someone or something. We want to acknowledge evil, but not let it win, as painful as it is.

The problem or pain is a way to ask God for help, knowing we are not alone and there's a force of good, mercy, and hope.

"Our spirit is our soul and houses the spark that is the God flame within us," he said. "It is the essence of our life, the living spirit of God. It is everything that is good in us that is not our body and mind. It is what motivates us and inspires us. It is what gives us hope. It is our real self. We are a spirit wearing a physical body.

"Faith is a recognition that we are not capable of doing good without the guidance and help of this presence that is the essence of all life," he said. "If we ignore that, we are merely treading water and not doing anything meaningful with our life.

"I ask for help every day," he said. "I pray that God will use me for a good purpose. I pray I will say the right word that can help a victim. I ask for protection and guidance. Faith is a constant recognition that He is there and that I am with Him. It's like having a partner in the patrol car."

The telephone rang and Willis glanced at the clock next to his bed. He'd been asleep about ninety minutes. A call like this—in the middle of the night—could only mean trouble, and within minutes Willis was dressed and out the door.

On the way to the crime scene, he thought about what had gone down: a 911 operator had taken a call from someone saying that a woman was screaming in a normally quiet neighborhood. Patrol units had been sent to investigate. On the way, they learned that the woman was barricaded in her home. Her ex-husband, armed with a shotgun, was outside demanding she open the door.

Soon, seven cops were on scene. From a block away they saw the man. He walked toward them, shotgun in his hand. They yelled at him to drop the weapon. He refused, raised his gun, and pointed it at the officers. They opened fire.

Even with light traffic, it took Willis more than an hour to arrive at the scene. He got a briefing: the dead man had told a neighbor he wanted to commit suicide by doing something that would make the cops kill him. The shotgun was empty.

Willis moved about the crime scene. The officers were being interviewed by detectives and other authorities. As righteous as the shooting was, Willis knew they'd feel guilty for taking a life.

He said a prayer for them.

Yellow tape held neighbors and spectators at bay. Willis lifted the tape and walked toward the dead man, who was lying in the middle of the intersection. By chance, he'd been shot and fallen directly under the only streetlight in the neighborhood. He stared at the man's body, the blood pooling underneath him.

Once again, he said a prayer.

Be at peace with God, he said. Be at peace.

The Message that points to Christ
on the Cross seems like sheer silliness
to those hellbent on destruction, but
for those on the way to salvation
it makes perfect sense.
This is the way God works, and most
powerfully as it turns out.

—1 Corinthians 1:18–21

"Here is the ultimate dialectic
between saving faith and rebellious reason.
Faith and reason were made compatible.
It's sin that broke up that unit.
And only the Gospel of Jesus Christ can
and does restore that true unit of faith and reason
under submission to the message of the Gospel."

—*Charles McIlhenny*

CHAPTER 15

Faith's Bookends

Charles McIlhenny glanced at his watch. In twenty-four hours his fate at Los Angeles County General, one of the busiest hospitals in the United States, would be decided by an administrator unhappy with the way he carried himself.

If the meeting ended poorly, McIlhenny could have his hospital privileges revoked. As much as he loved his job, McIlhenny couldn't change. To do so would not only be disingenuous, but it would violate everything he believed in.

Charles McIlhenny—a man who greeted everyone with a handshake, smile, or hug—was seen as a troublemaker because he openly believed in God and Jesus Christ. A hospital administrator, sensitive to patients who came from all faiths, or who had no faith, wanted McIlhenny to tone down the religion.

Instead of God, could McIlhenny use a more benign description? If you must pray, go ahead, but not in the name of Jesus Christ. The entire matter, McIlhenny thought, was ridiculous. As a Christian chaplain, who, exactly, was he supposed to pray to? He wasn't a Bible thumper or fundamentalist. But he certainly believed in Jesus Christ.

During a typical month he spoke with more than three hundred patients and their families. For those not of the

Christian faith, the hospital maintained a list of on-call chaplains of different faiths. If a patient or a patient's family wanted to talk with McIlhenny, he never preached or tried to convert. If someone said they weren't interested, he didn't take it personally. He didn't try to trick them into praying, dropping code words in their moment of fear to get them to believe what he believed. He wasn't trying to build up church membership or raise money for missionary work. But McIlhenny didn't hide his strong Christian beliefs. And in a crisis, he'd learned, most patients didn't seem to care.

A month earlier he had been making his rounds when he stopped to check on a man who'd been severely beaten. The man, recovering from a coma, had a brain injury. McIlhenny was about to leave when the patient's mother arrived. He introduced himself as a Christian chaplain. She didn't care what he was. All she asked was that McIlhenny pray for her son to recover.

McIlhenny had once wanted to be a doctor. But his father, a Baptist minister, convinced him to consider the ministry. Eventually McIlhenny earned a doctorate of ministry degree, led a church, and then retired. This chaplain's gig was a voluntary position. But McIlhenny had never felt as close to God as when he walked the hospital halls. The hospital, he liked to say, is where God drops off and picks up. Those bookends—life and death—cut to the heart of what faith is all about.

What is life? What is death?

At the hospital, everyone sought the answer. Nurses pulled him aside to seek a word of comfort, to inquire where God was during that horrible case in the emergency room.

Lunch over, McIlhenny stopped by his small cubicle to get the list of patients he would soon be visiting. As he walked down the hallway, he remembered the first autopsy he'd ever seen at the hospital. He'd stepped into a room, put on the gown and mask. Lying on the table was a sixty-four-year-old man who had died of pneumonia.

The doctors sliced the man open, pulled apart his chest, and took out his heart and body parts. To this day, McIlhenny remembers one specific detail—how the doctor used a soup ladle to scoop out the residue of blood and liquids. Two things struck him: how marvelous we are made and how the spirit had departed.

Those elements—soul and spirit—are so enigmatic and mysterious. Without them, the man can't move a muscle. The spirit, that vaporous thing, gives life to his body. With that spirit he marries, has children, and works a job.

An elevator door opened and McIlhenny stepped inside. As the doors closed, he thought of the autopsy.

How he wished that administrator could have stood there next to him in that autopsy room. How could he have then said there is no God after seeing the wonder of God's creation?

I was tagging along with a group of doctors when they stopped outside a room, conferred for a bit, and then pushed open the door to reveal a scene that, decades later, continues to haunt me. In the bed was a woman who appeared to be in her sixties. Thick white bandages about the size of a CD covered both eye sockets. A surgical team had removed both eyes. Cancer had taken them, and was now moving through her brain. The pain was unbearable. Even more so was the sound of her voice as she asked the question: Why was God doing this to her? She made a fist and pounded the mattress. As I left the room I heard her ask again, *why?*

That one word had propelled me for so long on this journey of faith. Why believe?

At times, when I was writing stories from the medical

world, I clearly felt God's presence in the surgeons and nurses. Getting them to talk about what they felt was difficult. They were wired differently, and thankfully so. I wanted my surgeon to be focused on the science and scalpel, not on questions that would intrigue a philosopher.

Yet when I watched surgeons at work, I was struck by the beauty and power of what they did. A surgeon's brain allowed her to operate on another human's brain. In their surgical scrubs, they embodied God. I saw fragility only once, and that was when I took a phone call from a doctor who wanted advice on what to say at the funeral for a patient. In that voice I heard a humanity, a sense of doubt, I'd not seen in the operating room.

During my travels I was lucky to meet Dr. Susan Winchester, an Alabama surgeon who was open about her faith and the role it plays in what she does. She considers being a doctor akin to priestly ministry. One afternoon, after a grueling day in the operating room, she attempted to explain to me that her faith gives her a center, a beginning, and an origin of hope.

Seeing the complexity of the body was, to her, overwhelming evidence of a creator. On the way to the hospital each morning, she said a simple prayer that encapsulated the Gospel: *Jesus, son of the living God, have mercy upon me, a sinner.*

A sinner? Her patients considered her a hero.

"All I am is a sinner," she said. "The same sinner you are. There's nothing great about me being a doctor that isn't true about any other person. My prayer is one of humility. It recognizes who Jesus is and asks for help and mercy."

Many of Dr. Winchester's patients are woman diagnosed with cancer. Not everyone will get cancer, but all of us will be hit by circumstances in life where we must confront and struggle with these great questions: Is there a God? Is God good? What is the basis of my sense of well-being and peace? Do I rely on circumstantial (external) or spiritual (internal) centeredness?

"It doesn't matter how many books you've written or what title is by your name," she said. "You're dealing with your own mortality. It pulls you back to your center. Where do I go for rest? Where do I go for peace? When I start to really focus on externals, what the world can give me, rather than knowing Jesus, I get completely out of sync with myself; it's a palpable and uncomfortable feeling."

Winchester said we must start with the acknowledgment that God is good—even when patients die. What God has for each of us, she said, is better than anything we can imagine. God's healing is sometimes a release from this earth.

"There's a time in every person's life where they say they're ready to leave this," she said. "They can't take the agony one more moment. They're ready to die, and I go to their bedside. I had a woman who asked me if I would just sing something to her. I believe that when you meld music with emotion, your intimacy with God and His spirit is at the maximum. So I sang a spiritual to her."

Her faith, she said, helps her see a patient's death not as her failure.

"If my practice is all about me succeeding, then I'm in a desperate and sad situation," she said. "I will be depressed and unable to heal, and healing is in part the relationship between the patient and me."

I asked her if she was afraid to die.

"I don't feel fearful," she said. "Maybe I will at the time it occurs. I hope I have the wisdom and peace. What God is doing in the world is like needlepoint. Look underneath and it looks like crap. Turn it over and there's a pattern made with all these pieces that look unrelated and sad and desperate."

Patients were waiting for her, but she wanted to leave me

with a thought about faith. She said it's a journey toward God and eternity, a walk that continues forever.

"For me it can be a minute-to-minute, hour-to-hour, day-by-day falling away and coming back," she said. "I think it happens purposely. I don't think God makes us fall away. I think we are enticed and seduced, come to a realization of our momentary separation, and then return to God and rest.

"You heard music in a black church and it lifted your soul, and you became aware of something else," she said. "You didn't know what the something else was, but it was a good feeling. The experience resonated with your center. I am supposed to encourage you, and you are supposed to encourage me. We are in the trenches of this world together. God has a plan."

I once watched a surgeon prep for a tough case involving a baby. I'd been in her office when she met the parents to explain what would happen in the operating room. I followed the surgeon, in her blue scrubs, as she went to meet with the parents one last time. When she disappeared into the pre-op room, I heard them say they had to go someplace important before the surgery began. They told one of the nurses they'd be in the hospital chapel.

Later, I visited the chapel, a small and windowless room. A Bible lay open to the book of Mark on a table. Near the door, also open, lay a prayer book. I flipped through the pages, reading the entries:

God, hear my prayers for my friend and for the other man who caused the accident.

My son has a severe brain injury, God. Please give him a chance to live a normal life.

Dear God, please help.

I stepped out of the chapel.

Did the people who came here believe?

Did they hope?

Were they foolish?

Faith while at church seems easy. But what about when you are at places where faith collides with the cruel realities of the world?

I waited near the hospital's security desk for McIlhenny, who told me he always wore a suit to work. Wait, he said, for someone who looks like an undertaker or business executive. I saw him in the distance, stopping every 10 feet or so to speak to a nurse, doctor, or employee. It seemed that everyone wanted a word with him. We set off through the hospital, and I asked what people wanted from him.

"Peace," he said. "I always tell people to read Proverbs. To work in a hospital, you need faith to deal with what you see and what you hear. Without faith, without believing in God, I think it would be impossible for these doctors and nurses to come to work day after day, shift after shift."

I told him that his role at the hospital reminded me of the chaplain in the television show *M*A*S*H* who struggled to maintain his own faith and help others—patients, doctors, and nurses—in the midst of carnage.

"I have to find comfort in God's word," he said. "Those words were made for me and everyone else. I still have to go through life's struggles. I think I have problems, but then I go to the hospital and meet the people there. My ego and self-centeredness shame me. Poor me. I have such a hard time. Then I go deal with these dear people. A seventeen-year-old girl was in a car accident and her mother was screaming. All I could do was hold her. God has used that—and so many other cases and people—to kick butt and say here is life. He gives me life and them life."

We walked down a hallway and a nurse stopped him. A security guard waved him over to talk and seek a word of comfort. As I stood listening to him, I knew that of all the people I'd met on my journey, McIlhenny was the most certain about faith, God, and Jesus Christ.

And I couldn't understand why.

Within this hospital people were dying. On floors above us, doctors were huddling, preparing to break the terrible news that the disease had spread too far and the outlook was terminal. In the emergency room, the staff prepared for a trauma case that would soon arrive, setting off a minute-by-minute battle to save a life.

As we continued walking, I asked McIlhenny to help me understand God's role in this building. He told me that faith is a gift of God, and he started using words that reminded me of those street preachers: *Bible*, *sinners*, *saved*, and *salvation*. Even as far along as I was on my own faith journey, something about those words reminded me of how off-putting faith can appear to those still questioning.

McIlhenny said that what he meant by faith being a gift, is if we accept that people are sinners, then we can't be saved by our own devices. That salvation is a gift of God. Faith, itself, he said, is a gift.

"I would argue that everyone has faith," he said. "The issue is not faith, but which faith? What is the direction and foundation of your faith? Then you have the development of your faith. I want to make myself clear on that.

"I love to talk to atheists," he said. "A few months ago I was on an airplane and God provided for me a wonderful atheist, a scientist. He was as convinced of his position as I was of mine, and we had a ball chatting about it for the four hours we were on the plane. But I have been through periods of doubt in terms of faith."

Doctors are among the most intelligent people I've met. A surgical specialty requires years of medical school, advanced training, and fellowships. What chance did faith have in a place full of so many brilliant people?

"It's like asking, why intellect?" McIlhenny said. "Why emotions? Why eyeballs? Why a foot? The ultimate answer is, that is what God gave us. That's who we are. We are creatures of God. Faith as much as anything is part of the makeup of an individual.

"The argument of whether you can believe in what you cannot see in terms of faith is bogus and comes from a secular philosophical viewpoint," he said. "Faith and knowledge as such are not dialectical in the slightest, any more than is knowledge and emotions, or knowledge and wearing glasses antithetical to faith."

The struggle—in the hospital or in the quiet of a home— he said, is twofold: toward God's word or against it, and our intellectual struggle over the issue.

"Struggling and growing up are all part of the faith process," he said. "I believe unbelievers are as much believers as I am. They have their god. Maybe it is with a small 'g.' No one is out there with no god, just swimming all by himself. He may think he is, but we all have our god and believe in that god— faith is fundamental to us as humans. As the Apostle Paul said, we either worship and serve the creature or we worship and serve the Creator.

"The theological idea—through Adam we fell in sin, and we now have that added feature of struggling against sin— there is an element within all of us that is fighting against God," he said. "We all struggle with that. And that struggle is an expression of our sinful rejection of God's authority over us.

It's not as if the atheist has settled the issue by denying God. I think the atheist struggles with faith and intellect as much as anyone else."

McIlhenny told me that faith is directed by God's word, not by our understanding of faith.

"Everyone struggles with those faith moments," he said. "It's not science versus faith, as such. Believers in God are gullible, they say. That statement itself is naive. That's a secular philosophical position that I disagree with. Some people have faith in reason, and reason becomes their god. The faith struggle is a part of faith living in a fallen world in a still morally corrupt body.

"God gave us tools: fingers and toes and even logical powers of reason," he said. "We have these tools, to use, to reason with, and then we ask, what directs our reason? Does it direct itself? Or is it directed by something else—someone from above or someone from below? I would say that it is always directed by someone. It is never on its own. Natural faith is the fundamental drive within us. But I need saving faith—not natural faith."

I told him I was confused.

"If I'm asked why I'm a Christian, I would say because God supernaturally made me that way," he said. "Through His word and my faith in Jesus—which is a gift of God—I see that He is the way.

"As a Christian," he said, "I believe in the powers of reason that God gave me. I am to be directed by the word of God, and so I use my reason—not as an end itself, but as under the direction of God's word. Reason is not the ultimate answer. Even faith is not the ultimate answer. Christ, or God in Christ, is the ultimate answer. Jesus is the reason God gives us for believing."

Weeks earlier, a radiologist walked up to McIlhenny in the

hospital cafeteria and told McIlhenny to give him the best argument for believing in Jesus Christ. McIlhenny—who loves such conversations—pushed aside his meal and talked about salvation and grace. The doctor, an agnostic, had so many questions. Questions, McIlhenny told him, were good. He reached into his pocket and handed the doctor his card. If the doctor ever wanted to talk, he knew where to reach McIlhenny. Before the doctor walked away, McIlhenny asked him a question: If there is no God, what is the point of all this? That, the doctor said, was what troubled him.

I told McIlhenny about my experiences, the other faith teachers, and how—while I'd resolved some faith questions—others had popped up.

"We need wisdom," he said. "We need godly wisdom from on high. Some people would argue that we need reason. I will counter that by saying that we don't find saving faith through natural reason but through wisdom from God.

"The book of Proverbs deals with the issue of finding this wisdom," he said. "Proverbs 2 asks all the questions Where? How? What? What does faith look and feel like? The Scriptures direct us toward the understanding of true wisdom from God. Yes, it's a faith issue. It's a reason and logic issue too."

The hospital was filled with brilliant minds. What is the difference between intelligence and wisdom, and how does faith fit into that?

"When we come to know who Jesus Christ is," he said. "He is the word of God personified. He is the essence of wisdom. That's what I have to grapple with. I still do. I'm still growing. I meet this character Jesus, the wisdom of God. I have to live by this supernatural faith in Him."

How much faith is necessary? I believed in Jesus and God. I had more faith now than I had ever had in my life. Could I quit my journey? How would I know when I was growing? When I started guitar lessons, it took months to learn how to make chords and strum a simple song. I improved dramatically, growing each week, then hit a plateau. How much did I need to learn? I was never going to be a professional musician. I just wanted to play guitar and be able to play a few songs.

I didn't want to be a pastor or church leader. I'd studied faith as a skeptic—looking for more reasons not to believe than believe—and I was a believer. Was that good enough? Could I call it quits?

"Jesus answers that," he said. "How much faith do you need? Jesus answers by saying that even faith the size of a mustard seed can root up trees and move mountains. As I read it, it's not how much faith you have but what the object of that faith is. The question is, how do you use that saving faith?

"In terms of the mustard seed–size faith and moving mountains, frankly, I have no need to move mountains as such," he said. "If I can pay my mortgage, I'm happy. The exaggeration—moving mountains—is there because it directs me to the power of God-directed faith, which rests in what God can do. It is so enormous."

If I were sitting in church on a Sunday, I'd buy that, even consider it the makings of a great sermon. But this hospital was like being at the front during a war where even the strongest of faiths would seem to be shaken.

"I love it," he said. "I'm dealing with life and death at every moment. Today I had a male patient who was in the ICU just gasping and clinging to life. I love to be with such people on the brink of eternity. It's exhilarating to be there and literally lead them to the threshold of heaven.

"Maybe I can't say anything to the patient," he said. "Maybe I can't do anything for him. Maybe all I can do is hold his hand, whisper to him, and pray and read scripture. I was with a family today in ICU whose mother was dying. She was on the verge of entering eternity. And then I worked with newborn babies today.

"Death and birth," he said. "Birth and death."

Perhaps no place is as lonely as a waiting room where loved ones wait for news from a doctor. A cop, like Lt. Dan Willis, could answer one part of the great why question—where the crime or accident took place, how the justice system was mobilizing to do something, take action to try and right a wrong. I'd been in hospital chapels, read the guest book, and seen the prayer requests, and the question of why is more profound. How could McIlhenny respond to a question of why life seems so unfair and why God's power seems to be used so arbitrarily?

"It depends on their state of mind," he said. "Some are crying out 'Why me?' If they are really interested, the Bible gives a variety of answers. Some you will like, some you will not. And I will never judge the value of why a person is crying out. The psalms are filled with the question of fairness and why the wicked seem to get fat and happy and the good die young.

"Why, God?" he asked. "I will tell people that fundamentally we, way back in the beginning, rebelled against God. God warned us. The fool screws up his life and then blames God. That's what we do and so quickly blame God. Sin brought death. We suffer because of sin. Life comes across as unfair."

The very first dead body I saw as a young reporter was a man who'd been going to work when a drunk, headed the wrong way on the freeway, slammed into his car. I still remember the man's yellow tie, his wedding ring, and how it could have been me—just a regular guy who kisses his wife good-bye in the morning and is commuting to work when his life ends. What, I asked McIlhenny, about the truly innocent victim?

"I have that struggle," he said. "We had a female patient, twenty-seven, a single mother with an eight-year-old daughter. She was in the hospital for kidney stones and was given medicine that reacted so violently that it killed her extremities. She had to have her arms and legs cut off to survive. It wasn't her fault. I had to minister to her when a medical accident was ruining her present life."

How, I asked, could he do that?

"I am there because God has called me to this," he said. "I like to be with people like that. In fact, I prayed with her quite often. I wanted to learn how I could minister to her and give her comfort. She is a human being made in the image of God. She deserved my attention with all the God-given skills I could muster on her behalf."

"She believed in God," he said. "I turned her experience into a lesson for me. I am so very grateful for the challenge God gave me through her tragedy. I had to say to her, you now have to raise your daughter without arms and legs, and God will provide for you every step of the way."

"It's interesting how God somehow answers our needs," he said. "That seems unreasonable to the unbeliever. I don't know where God's answer will come from. He will provide someone to come alongside."

It seemed to me believers give God a pass. When something bad happens, it's because we have sinned and God has nothing to do with it. When something good happens, God gets all the praise.

I told McIlhenny I'd once profiled a cardiac surgeon who helped invent the artificial heart valve and performed the world's first triple-valve replacement. That valve has allowed more than 350,000 people to cheat death. One of his patients told me she was seventeen when she came down with what she thought was flu. Doctors discovered her heart valve had collapsed and needed to be replaced. Without it, she was told, she had less than six months to live. Now married, she is not only a mother, but a grandmother. The surgeon saved her life, not God.

"Yes, and he had a God-given ability in him to make that valve for her," he said. "If I deny that—if I say I love my body and deny the one who made me—that is the ultimate insult to my creator. It is the height of arrogance to honor the tool and ignore the creator. So it is with honoring and worshipping the tool—logic and man's own mental powers—while dishonoring God, who made it.

"Our ego gets in the way of faith and screws us up," he said. "It messes with faith and redirects us away from God. We are God's instruments."

I admitted that I sometimes struggled with my own ego. I wrote the story. But I realize the way I see the world, and people, is a gift from God.

"Tonight, I want you to go to Psalm 139," he said. "Read it. It points out who I am, who Tom is. When we hang on to our ego, we begin to believe that we are the creator and then our faith lies within what we can do."

In the end, I asked, why does faith matter? We will all die. Is faith something society needs so we'll be on our best behavior? Is it a way of pacifying ourselves, a way to find comfort in a cruel world?

"Death is not the end," he said. "Death is a moment in life. Then there's the resurrection. The resurrection on the last day means that our work is over and we don't have to go through this life and its struggles again. Christ answers that He is the resurrection and the life. When you die with faith in your heart for Christ, you also live forever. My faith accepts that or rejects it. Either way, I have faith."

If it's so attractive, the end so glorious, why doesn't God

tell us where we're going at the start of the journey? Why make life so tough?

"God exercises our faith by putting us through the valley of the shadow of death," he said. "In the hospital I use the twenty-third psalm all the time. Why go through all that exercise? At my age, I feel terrible after an hour of weight lifting. But the next day I feel so good.

"Faith is where it aches," he said. "People and circumstances in your life will exercise your faith. You get depressed. People try your patience. God brings faith to life. Then you get through the exercise, and God brings you out of it."

"Faith is where it aches."

So should I look at life, those tough times, like lifting weights? Is life a series of faith lessons?

"God has a lesson for you," he said. "We have to constantly see the big picture—life and death. In that moment of grief, sometimes we don't want to see it. I was part of a case where one person said God was going to raise this victim up. After fourteen weeks I had to talk to the wife. She had to give him over to God.

"Read Proverbs, start with chapter one," he said. "It tells you the secret of living forever. Let it speak to you. Let it challenge you. If it is really God's Word, only He can demonstrate it."

The meeting in the administrator's office lasted more than two hours. Everyone agreed that McIlhenny was an outstanding chaplain. He'd received no complaints from patients or staff. Hospital officials agreed that he could maintain his privileges.

He continued on his rounds. Several Muslim employees

asked him questions about the Bible. And a radiologist who'd asked McIlhenny to give him the best argument for Christ said he wanted to continue the conversation.

As he made his rounds, he thought of a recent patient. The woman had an advanced case of MS and could move only her eyes, blinking them when he pointed to a letter in the alphabet. But her mind was intact, and McIlhenny had conversations about God, the Bible, and life.

One day she told McIlhenny she wanted to profess her faith in Jesus Christ as her personal savior. She did so arduously, blinking and blinking while he stood by her bedside, holding a Bible in his hand. She said she wanted to be baptized. He performed the ritual.

Less than twenty-four hours later, she died from a massive infection.

His work was complete.

This is what the LORD says to his anointed,
to Cyrus, whose right hand I take hold of
to subdue nations before him
and to strip kings of their armor,
to open doors before him
so that gates will not be shut:
I will go before you
and will level the mountains;
I will break down gates of bronze
and cut through bars of iron.
I will give you hidden treasures,
riches stored in secret places,
so that you may know that I am the LORD,
the God of Israel, who summons you by name.

—Isaiah 45:1–3

"This scripture encourages my heart greatly.
It makes me aware of the fact that God knows my situation.
It also empowers me by letting me know that
God will make a way for me, despite the obstacles.
He will break down the bars of iron and the gates of brass,
and He will level the mountains.
He will give me the treasures I need to fulfill
his purpose and do his will.
He knows me by name."

—*Pastor Mark Strong*

CHAPTER 16

My Pastor

When he had a free moment—his four children all wanted something at the same time—Pastor Mark Strong pulled aside his wife and told her he was overwhelmed and wondered if he was the right man to lead the church. That he even was a pastor would surprise the kids he grew up with.

His mother took him to church and Sunday school where he learned about God and Jesus: at ten he felt so close to God that he was baptized. The thrill wore off days later and he drifted from church. During his teen years, he was into the party life and girls. In the back of his mind God existed, but not in terms of being personally connected to Him. He prayed before meals and before going to sleep but had no awareness of God during the day. His mother spoke of God's love and mercy, but it meant nothing to Strong.

Then a nineteen-year-old friend—the same age as he was—had heart failure and died. No one close to Strong had died, and he grappled with the concepts of life and death. His search for answers—why his friend, a good kid who led a good life?—was fruitless. In his grief, nothing made any sense or gave him comfort.

With his brothers and friends, he attended his friend's funeral and watched the casket be carried out of the church and

loaded into a hearse. Services over, his friends went back to
the life: music on, rolling with the boys, and smoking weed.
Something, though, had changed in Strong. He told his friends
to stop. Didn't they know what had happened? They told him
he was tripping. Relax. What's wrong with you?

On the Sunday before Christmas, his grandmother invited
him to church. He attended because he wanted her off his
back. If he went one Sunday, he'd get one or two months of
peace without her bugging him. Church services ran from
eleven to noon, and with fifteen minutes to go, Strong's aunt,
an opera singer home for the holidays, walked in.

Strong knew this appearance was going to drag the service out another forty-five minutes because she'd be asked to
sing, But about three-quarters of the way through her song,
Strong found himself standing and crying. There was no altar
call or invitation by the pastor. It wasn't even part of the service.

But he stood and said out loud, "God, if you want me, you
can have me."

So many times people say that when they give their life to
God, it gets better.

Strong's got worse.

I'd been on a roll at work. Months earlier I'd finished a series about a young Portland attorney who'd argued in front of
the U.S. Supreme Court, and I'd received great reader reaction. And this morning's paper featured my story of a woman
who had been confined to a wheelchair after an accident but
refused to let the wheelchair define her life. This woman inspired me, and the telephone calls I received showed that readers felt that way too.

When the phone rang again, I heard a friend's voice:

What's your car doing in the paper? And so started a storm that battered my life, knocked me to me knees, and ultimately revealed to me a new side of faith.

A decade earlier I'd immersed myself in the life of a Portland high financier who at one time was worth $100 million. I'd written a seven-part series that won a national writing award detailing what happened when he lost it all as his business collapsed.

He turned out to be one of the most controversial figures in Portland, Oregon, ended up doing time in federal prison, and his business ethics were a source of continued debate and discussion. I knew none of that when I was writing my human interest story. I spent nearly a year with him. We traveled across the country and spent hundreds of hours together as he gave me access to his personal and professional life.

Years later, in passing, he offered me a spot at his company's lot, where he allowed his employees, his kids, and their friends to park for free. He had plenty of open spaces. Without giving it much thought, I said yes.

Even though I hadn't written about him since the series—and we both knew I would never again write about him—the inference was that by getting a "free" parking spot I could be seen as compromising journalistic ethics. The local alternative weekly paper was tipped to where I was parking. A photographer took a picture of my car, and that paper ran a contest asking readers to identify to whom the car belonged. After hanging up the phone, I tracked down a copy of the paper. There it was.

I walked into my boss's office and told him what I'd discovered. Up the chain it went. After years of being a private man in the office and taking my job seriously, my integrity was now in question. Hours later I was sent home to wait while my fate was decided. By then the alternative paper ran a story, of course, on the "contest." My personal and professional life had just become very public. I suddenly felt embarrassed, alone, and vulnerable.

Two days later I got a call telling me to come into the paper. I thought walking into the building lobby was the hardest thing I'd done in my life. I was wrong. The hardest was walking through the newsroom—a marked man—as I made my way to a corner office where the punishment was handed out: time off and my title—senior reporter—taken away.

That night my wife and I were supposed to attend a party with our ballroom dance group. I dressed in my tuxedo and put on an act, not sure who knew what was going on in my life or what to say. In a past life, I would have pretended nothing was wrong. I was the guy who didn't tell anyone for decades that his parents had divorced.

That night—while all around me people were doing the fox-trot—I made a leap of faith as bold as anything I'd done in my life. I walked over to a man who I knew had a deep faith, and told him what was going on. I asked him to pray for me, and he said he would.

That Sunday I came to church early and waited until Pastor Mark Strong pulled into the parking lot. I cornered him, his suit jacket still slung over his shoulder, and told him what had happened. He wrapped an arm around me and prayed right there, next to his car, while church members made their way inside the building. Before leaving me, he told me to read a particular section in the book of Job—the section of the Bible that once changed Annette Steele's life.

Everyone seemed to be having a better Sunday than I was. The service and sermon did nothing for me. That night, I picked up my Bible and read the passage suggested by Pastor Strong:

All I want is an answer to one prayer,
a last request to be honored:
Let God step on me—squash me like a bug,
and be done with me for good.
I'd at least have the satisfaction
of not having blasphemed the Holy God,
before being pressed past the limits.
Where's the strength to keep my hopes up?
What future do I have to keep me going?
Do you think I have nerves of steel?
Do you think I'm made of iron?
Do you think I can pull myself up by my bootstraps?
Why, I don't even have any boots.

—Job 6:8–13

Damn right. At that moment, that was my life.

On Tuesday, I called the church to see if Pastor Strong was around. While on hold, I thought about hanging up, but I had nowhere else to turn. Then he came on the line. I asked if I could come see him sometime that week.

On Sunday—when he stands before so many people—Pastor Mark Strong is a maestro leading an orchestra. His words, voice, and even his body language are tools he uses to reach the hearts and souls.

He was my pastor, and I expected him to entertain and inspire me. He was part teacher and part performer, but it wasn't until I had sat in his office that I saw him not just as Pastor Mark, but as Mark, a man not unlike myself. In him, I saw parallels with my own life. To some people I wasn't Tom, I was a reporter and I'd come to represent all that was good and bad with the media. I didn't want that burden. And neither, I was sure, did Pastor Strong. We met in the middle of the week, sitting at a table just outside the doors that led into the sanctuary.

"I have my struggles," he said. "To admit that helps me to stay dependent on God. It also helps me stay sensitized. Can you imagine leading people if you've never had any struggles, battles, or doubts? That's a recipe for disaster. My turmoil keeps my feet on the ground and turned the right way."

When I started coming to church, I looked at faith as similar to getting a vaccination to protect me from life's problems. I'd since learned that I'd been foolish. At one level, my life hadn't improved. Yet on another, I was a better man, more thoughtful and with less of an ego and belief that I could control my destiny.

I still grappled with the unfairness of life and why my faith didn't tip the scales to give me an advantage. I juggled bills and old cars, while friends had been blessed with more money than I'd ever see.

Couldn't God cut me a break?

"It's not always easy," Strong said. "I've had this eye problem that has baffled doctors for the last two years. I've been told that a couple of drops will take care of it. Then surgery was supposed to be the answer.

"Do I like it?" he asked. "No.

"Do I understand it?" he said. "No."

For a moment, he was preaching.

"Then a lady in our church had the same situation," he said. "She was scheduled for the same surgery I had. Then God healed her. She didn't have to go through the things that I had to endure. The day of the surgery, the pressure in her eyes was normal. Of course I'm rejoicing for her. But at the same time, I wonder about me. Why not me?"

Given that, are there times when you feel God's absence? Here you are doing His work, helping people find their way to

God, and He's not there for you. At what point does being a pastor become less about your relationship with God and more of a job where your boss doesn't seem to appreciate you and hasn't given you a raise?

"There have been times in my life where I had a drought that lasted as long as two years," he said. "There are times when I say, *God, where are You?* But during those times, I go on what I know. I believe the Scriptures. I believe that God is there.

"I may not have all the emotions or feelings that I'd like to have," he said. "It's always easier when I have them. But I still believe God is who He says He is. I need to be authentic in my faith journey. I need to be authentic, too, about church. There is no perfect place or perfect church. People come to church for relief. They want to get their problems solved and difficulties taken care of. I can't blame them. That's some of the reason I go to church."

He pointed beyond the double doors to a room that would be filled with people come Sunday.

"But it's important for people to realize that we are all in the process of growing in faith," he said. "That means tensions and disagreements. What we need to focus on in faith is that we may not be where we want to be, but at least we are not where we were."

Each Sunday, Pastor Strong liked to end the service by inviting people to join the church. He wasn't selling as much as inspiring. Not a week went by that at least one person didn't make that commitment. Some people, after coming just three times, joined.

I asked him what happened when he stood up that Sunday so long ago.

"From that moment my life was drastically altered and changed," he said. "Was I perfect? Absolutely not. But there was a change. First and foremost I knew a reality of God that I'd never known before. We never know when we will realize that truth. It can happen in church or when we're talking with someone. It can come when we're actively searching, or it can come when we don't think we're ready."

How did he know he was ready, and not just caught up in the emotion of the moment? His story—and watching others join the church—reminded me of when I'd gone to a car dealer to look at cars. The sale, the pitch and hustle, started the moment I walked in the door. How would I—or anyone contemplating responding to a similar message about God— know when we're ready?

"If I had to boil it down, it was that I knew to the depths of my heart and soul that God loved me," he said. "I knew that Christ was not someone you read about in the Bible. He was not just a picture on the wall, or a character in a Sunday-morning message."

That seemed as if it would be obvious for anyone—aside from Sunday school kids—who attended church. Pastor Strong smiled and agreed. But he wanted to emphasize a subtle difference in how Jesus is perceived.

"He is the risen," Pastor Strong said, trying to get me to understand what changed for him. "He is the living God and is alive in my life. Based on all that, my life went through a transformation. I changed the way I thought and conducted myself. I changed the way I spoke. I changed what was in my heart.

"You've talked about the faith struggle," he said. "I relate. I had to figure out what to do with my goals and desires, and figure out what God wanted for my life. The journey of faith differs from person to person. You often hear people say that when they give God their life, it gets better. Well, mine got incredibly worse. There was more confusion, more difficulty, and more sacrifice."

Pastor Strong said he died a symbolic death, shedding the old Mark Strong. Even though God's presence in his life was a reality, he went through a three-year period where he felt as if he were in the desert. The parts of his old life that he so enjoyed—the weed, the girls, and old friends who were a bad influence—vanished; they had to if he was to become the man God wanted him to be.

"It wasn't easy," he said. "I didn't instantly change with a snap of my fingers. The only way I was able change was through God's strength. When people talk about what faith means, I think my life is a perfect example. I didn't know where I was headed or why. I was walking into uncertainty. There were many reasons for me not to take that step, to turn back. Faith is what made it possible for me to continue."

If faith is so critical to a life well led, why don't we hear God's call? If God is all-powerful, why doesn't He speak loudly to get our attention?

"Our lives are so busy," he said. "There's so much noise surrounding us. The bills we have to pay, the situations we need to work out, the jobs that are a struggle, and the relationships that have issues. The way we were raised and our insecurities that come from that. Plus vulnerability, pride, and ego. All that adds up to tremendous noise that makes it hard to hear God's call to faith.

"Take a radio station that broadcasts on a frequency of 1530," he said. "You can't get it if you tune your radio to 1490. I believe the way you dial into God is by hearing His call through all the noise. God enables you and gives you the grace to hear Him. But I don't think He forces people to do it.

"If a person has a willingness to hear the calling of faith, they can dial into the frequency," he said. "Once you do that, you're able to hear what God is saying to your heart. It may not be some mammoth thing. It may be one little piece, just one bit of information or self-disclosure from God that transforms your life."

I knew that Pastor Strong had seen me in the back row for years. I'd been in his office, a broken man who he'd help find the tools to move on in life. I'd attended church events and volunteered to be part of a work crew. Yet I'd never joined this church—his church. He'd never asked me why not, never twisted my arm or made me feel guilty. He never treated me any differently.

I sensed—that favorite word of mine—that joining the church would be an important part of my faith journey. But I couldn't do it. Why do some people, not feeling brave enough to admit I was talking about myself, resist surrendering to faith?

"Jesus said that men do not want to come into the light because their deeds are evil," he said. "They like the darkness and ignorance. We believe too much in our own understanding and reasoning. The spiritual life doesn't work that way. Yes, we use our minds. Yes, we reason. But when we look at the way we're made up, it's a combination of mind, body, soul, and spirit. All those are different components that God has given us. It is in how we use them that allows us to connect to God.

"If you have a computer and are running a software program for a MAC and try to use a PC program, it won't work," he said. "There are certain components that the PC will not be able to read. When we talk about spiritual life, there are certain things that a natural man won't be able to receive because they are written for a spiritual man."

Many people, he said, see people of faith as having to live by rules: do this; don't do that. In one sense, he said, they're correct. But those rules lead to a more fulfilling life.

"People from the outside don't realize how good the faith life is," he said. "Life is complex, and there are many things we don't have answers to. But God does two things: He offers an unspeakable joy, and He offers a peace that passes all understanding. Faith in God gives us a peace for those times we can't understand.

"You develop and cultivate your relationship with Him," Pastor Strong said. "It's not just what we do. Yes, we have to put the hoe in the ground and cultivate. But at the same time, God is interested in cultivating our relationship with Him."

What about people who say they already have a good life? They're kind, help others, and attempt to live by the Golden Rule.

He said it annoys him when people say they're helping people, especially the less fortunate. Faith, he emphasized, isn't a matter of measuring ourselves in terms of how we treat our fellow man. We need faith because God is the creator and we have to be in right relationship with Him.

"Not out of coercion or force, but out of love and His grace," Pastor Strong said. "Faith is asking, How do I stand up before God? The truth is, we all fall short. That's when Jesus comes in."

How do you sell faith and a relationship with Christ? If you tell me that I'll lose weight by working out, I can see the results, which motivates me to continue working toward a goal. I change my diet and take steps instead of the elevator. I may crave pizza, but I know exactly what I'll get if I pass on the slice and order a salad instead. But faith is more mysterious. How do I measure where I am on my journey? It's not like I get to wake up one day and realize that my pants suddenly fit better.

"I can tell you that there are markers along the way," he said. "They are individual markers. Yours will be different than mine. But by being aware, by looking back, we see where we have come from."

I told him that if I was to graph my faith journey, it would look like the 2011 stock market—soaring highs and plunging lows. Yes, there were moments—even entire days—when I saw the absolute necessity of faith, church, and God in my life. Some Sundays I didn't feel it, and I'd grudgingly go to church. Or I'd just hang, read the paper, watch football, and not feel at all guilty.

"The truth is that faith is messy," he said. "It's not an easily told story that has a definite beginning, middle, and end. It's not a television show that wraps up everything in a neat ending by the end of the hour.

"Yes, we put our faith in concrete things. We trust in God. We believe in Christ. We know our sins are forgiven. But walking that faith is a mystery," he said. "If everything was all calculated and planned to the second, you'd never know or begin to understand faith. Faith is much like life in that you never know what turns will appear in the road or where your journey will take you. Faith says that, regardless of the path, I—and you—will trust God. And somehow, as you engage in the situation, you will come out of it.

"Most importantly, faith is not what you get out of it in terms of material things and a so-called easy life," he told me. "But you will have acquired information and knowledge about God that will help you grow closer to Him. As you go through the stages of life—the good and the difficult times—you will get to know God.

"As you journey with God, you learn more about Him," he said. "As you learn more, you gain not just knowledge in your head, but in your heart. Through that—through faith—you are transformed."

Does it matter if I continue to feel that tug between what seem to be two so different approaches—my intellect and my heart? I'd prayed, read the Bible, and come to church, all things I considered emotionally based actions. But I still wanted to understand faith, to be able to break it down in the way a chef could if I asked her to explain the fine main course she'd just served me.

"Faith does not just hit you emotionally or mentally," he said. "Faith hits you in the center and core of who you are as a person. Since faith exists in the depth of who you are, there are times when faith will manifest itself cognitively and times when faith manifests itself emotionally.

"That's part of the faith process and journey," he said. "What happens is that faith and God are brought to bear on your total being. What are you, Tom? A man, a husband, a father, a friend, a musician, and a writer. And I'm just talking about a few of the pieces that make you who you are. We're all like that with multiple parts that make us who we are.

"Faith touches all parts of us," he told me, "sometimes at different times in our life and at times that make no sense and in ways that can be confusing to us."

What is the faith journey?

"First of all, by no means have I arrived at the end of my faith journey," he said. "I don't want to give that impression. I'm still a work in progress, still learning like everyone else. But what I have discovered is that while God can easily give answers, He delights in the process just as much as the final answer.

"We learn our lessons along the way," he said. "That makes them more meaningful. We understand them at a deeper level than if we were told exactly what to do, how to do it, and why to do it. Faith does not protect us from life. People of faith have to live their lives like everyone else. What faith does is give us perspective about life."

Is faith dependent on a church?

"God is a God of community," he said. "God has always

been about a community of people. Community is His church. In different places and cultures, church looks different. But at its core, church is a gathering of people. There are myths and stereotypes about church, including that the church or pastor just wants your money. Sure there are some charlatans out there, and some criticism is deserved. Yes, you can come to church and find unethical people, just like when you go to an office, college, or any institution.

∽∾∽

"God is a God of community."

"But I would not be where I am now without people," he said.

He made me think about a woman I'd talked to from New York City. A cocaine addict on welfare, she was taking care of three children while her husband was doing time in prison. In prison he joined a Christian fellowship group led by people from the outside. One of the men who visited him belonged to a church near her apartment. The man reached out to her, but she pushed him away, wanting nothing to do with God.

One Christmas Eve she had nothing for her three kids. She'd sold everything to get drugs for herself. She heard a knock on the door, opened it, and saw a deliveryman holding a box. Inside the apartment she opened the box and found Christmas presents. The fellowship group had bought toys for the children.

At the sight of the gifts, she began weeping. Why, she asked herself, would these people help a broken-down drug addict? For the first time in her life, she thought about God. Maybe He was using people to do His work.

Desperate, and with her children beside her, she prayed: "If you really are a God in heaven, then do a miracle. Not later, right now. I'm tired and my kids are in danger. I want a different life. God, I give myself to You."

The next day she called the man from the fellowship group. He sent someone to take her to church. When the service ended, the pastor told her that Jesus Christ had died for her and all she had to do was accept that forgiveness and then ask Jesus to help her live a changed life. They prayed together.

The church helped get her into vocational school. They sent a van every week to take her and the kids to church. They took her to visit her husband. They sent her kids to Bible camp. They helped her stay off drugs and opened their homes to her. With the people from church, she felt God's presence.

He was there in the smallest of things—when she'd bring the kids to church and find members had made breakfast for them. When her husband was released from prison, the two of them rebuilt a life on a foundation of Christ. They both got jobs, stayed clean, and went to church. More than twenty years have passed since her life changed that Christmas Eve. As powerful as God was, she came to Him by people who showed her the way.

"You cannot make the Christian walk alone," Pastor Strong said after I told him the story. "Yes, we each have our own personal relationship with God. Prayer is a communication with God. You disclose your heart to God, and He discloses His heart to you. It's a dialogue. But that relationship flourishes in the context of the church community."

As uplifting as those stories can be—and every church has some variation of that tale—I asked Pastor Strong if faith, as good as it could be, was ever personally burdensome. And what about a lack of answers?

"I can tell you what the Bible says," he told me. "I can encourage you. I can love you. But ultimately your answer and help have to come from God. What I don't want to do as a pastor is create a dependency on me. Faith is not a dependency on others, but a dependency on God. When we have dependency on God, we can depend on others, but we can't put the cart before the horse. If I create a dependency on me, then I'm doing the people a disservice. We need to learn to depend on God. All of our interactions go through Him. Then we draw from each other."

Why had I been sent to this church on assignment so long ago?

"Someone has to be able to articulate a voice," he said. "How can a person hear faith? Or the voice of God? Go back to the radio station I spoke of. There has to be a disc jockey to put music on the airwaves so people have the opportunity, if they tune to the right frequency, to hear it. I believe that you are a person God is using to do that.

"Your words and conversations are rest stops on the faith journey," he said. "It's a place where we can pause and nurture our spirit. It's a place where we can think and feel, question, ponder, and seek. It's a way to start a conversation between a husband and wife who don't know how to talk about faith in a way that has meaning. It's a way for a parent to talk with a child about faith, or a child to a parent.

"God," he said, "will lead someone to these pages."

I was at my lowest point in life since I had been fired from my job in New York City. I rose from the table we'd been sitting at and slowly followed Pastor Mark Strong into his office. He sat in a chair next to mine, said a prayer, and said it was time to talk—in faith. For the next hour we talked about God, disappointment, and the shock that comes when a man is forced to look at his life with utter clarity.

The day I came back to work, I decided to do it alone. I

kissed my wife good-bye, told her I would be fine—even though I wasn't sure what awaited me—and set out walking from my house to the paper.

On the way, I listened to Stevie Ray Vaughn—the fiery blues guitarist—attempting to channel his intensity and take-no-prisoners attitude. I remembered the time I'd entered a karate tournament and felt my legs tremble as I looked across the mat at my strong and more experienced opponent. I tried to channel my fighting spirit—no fear—and capture what it felt like when I beat the man.

Nothing worked.

I stood outside the newspaper's doors and looked into the lobby. I turned off the CD player and wondered if I had what it took to take the next step.

It was then that I prayed.

I asked God to give me the strength to walk through those doors, take the elevator to the fourth floor, walk across the newsroom—knowing everyone was looking at me—and take a seat at a new desk with a new assignment, mourning what had been and what would never be again.

I opened the door and stepped inside.

Months later, I arrived early for church one Sunday and avoided Pastor Strong, who was in an outer hallway. The man knew my secrets and fears. He'd borne witness to my anger and sadness. I sat half-heartedly in my seat, not at all sure if I'd return the next week.

Why had I come back to this church following the assignment years earlier?

I had told myself that I found faith alluring, but it also scared me. Faith—if I truly embraced it—would force me to remove the mask I so easily wore. I needed something in my life that was bigger than me, something more than an accumulation of awards, a title, and résumé that I'd allowed to define me and my life's purpose. As painful as the process had been, I'd received what I had asked for.

I stood, made my way through people coming into the church, and walked into the hallway to find Pastor Strong.

"Thank you," I said. He knew what I was talking about.

He hugged me.

I returned to my seat.

Now what?

I'm not saying that I have this all together,
that I have it made.
But I am well on my way, reaching out for Christ,
who has wondrously reached out for me.
Friends, don't get me wrong:
By no means do I count myself an expert in all of this,
but I've got my eye on the goal,
where God is beckoning us onward—to Jesus.
I'm off and running, and I'm not turning back.

—Philippians 3:12–14

"Coming from where I've been,
this passage always has a place in my heart.
It's not about what I have already attained
or that I am already perfected.
What it means, to me, is that I press on,
reaching for what was in front of me."

—*Joshua Polk*

CHAPTER 17

Redemption

The cell phone on the nightstand rang and Joshua Polk woke up in an instant. None of this groggy, where-am-I nonsense. A man survives prison by learning to sleep like a cat, ready to react in a second. He glanced at the clock—3:00 a.m.—and then at the caller ID, recognizing his son's number.

Over the years Polk had shed many a tear for his son. So many times he'd prayed to God, asking that his twenty-five-year-old child not end up in trouble with the law, the way he had. He answered the phone.

"Dad, I messed up bad. Come see me."

He got the address to a low-rent motel room on a seedy avenue miles from his home where he lived with his wife. Polk told his son he'd be there as soon as possible. He encountered little traffic as he headed east and let his mind wander, thinking about his own life and how he'd so easily drifted into trouble. His life could be measured with a line—before and after. He didn't want that to happen to his son.

When he was growing up, Polk's mother took him to a church that had a strong youth movement. Hanging out with other kids was the initial attraction, but at some point—and he'd never been able to pinpoint exactly when or how—he developed what he considered a personal relationship with God.

Never a shy kid, Polk talked openly with his friends, even non-believers, about Jesus and faith. Some were interested. Others tolerated it. A few thought all this church talk was crazy.

After crossing a few intersections, Polk slowed his car to look for the motel. With a tug on the wheel, he turned his car into the lot. In front of him he saw a balcony packed with men. He assumed that was the room where his son was hiding.

Members of the group—gangbangers and wannabes—stared down at him, wondering if he was a cop or just an easy mark. He knew their type. He'd met them in the prison recreation yard, where a man learns to be aware of his surroundings and carry himself with a confidence that says "back off and mind your own business."

On any Sunday, Polk could pray and sing with the best of them. But he carried with him a bit of the street. Even when he started dealing marijuana, people told him he seemed different from other dealers. Polk told his customers they saw the mark of God on him.

Along the way, something changed. Money and drugs, maybe a grab for power and a desire to have a different kind of immortality. Out on the street a man could live forever if he had enough juice. He moved up to dealing cocaine, and the money came rolling in with the good times right behind.

Within the group lurked an informant, and everyone got swept up in a big-time federal drug investigation. When the trial ended, Polk got 151 months in prison—more than twelve years, the time it takes a child to go through school and finish off freshman year in college. He was in his thirties, and his family was disappointed because they had so much hope for him. His son, the young man he was now going to see, was just a little guy when Daddy went away.

Polk yanked the key from the ignition and opened the car door. When he shut it, the sound echoed off the motel. The balcony crowd gave him a hard look that said they meant business. Thing was, he meant business too.

He stood next to his car and prayed: "I'm hurting, God. Whatever befalls me, be there for me."

And then Joshua Polk went looking for his son.

Still reeling from my work problems and trying to find my way in a world where the landscape had changed so dramatically, I tried to remember what I learned about myself—not when I'd won the Pulitzer Prize, but when I'd lost.

Losing had been a more profound experience. I had been forced to shed parts of myself—clear my head and heart—and trust in the power of story. And now, in much the same way, I had to trust in the power of faith.

What struck me was that faith—at its core—was not just about the church and my pastor and all the trappings we impose on faith as a way to give it structure. Faith, at least the way I saw it, was an opportunity to turn away from myself and seek out a higher power. In these moments—often in times of doubt—there's a barrenness that's necessary for growth. Was God putting me through the ringer for a reason?

Faith steps don't always come at the optimal time. Yes, it would be perfect to find faith on Easter Sunday and let it build and grow through Christmas Day. But that wasn't realistic. I thought, of all things, about a vacation my family had taken years earlier. We'd been driving from Portland to Los Angeles when the transmission on our minivan went out in Redding, California. At the time, it seemed a disaster, but it turned out to be the best vacation our family ever had. What I'd learned about faith during my journey and my conversations was that while faith couldn't change dire circumstances, it allowed me to respond differently to those circumstances.

I found comfort in knowing that Jesus Christ—a real man—had experienced everything I'd gone through: anger, rejection, and feeling like an outcast. He knew and understood. Years earlier, I would have scoffed at such a foolish statement. But now it made sense to me. It was also at that moment when what I had long considered to be faith's separate components—the head and the heart—joined forces.

Weeks later I noticed in the church bulletin that the men's group was holding a Saturday breakfast. Something compelled me to go. When breakfast ended, Joshua Polk got up in front of the group to tell us his story, and it made me think about what had happened to me at work. I'd been filtering all areas of my life through the experience that had happened to me. I didn't want to talk about what I was feeling, or going through, but I had to fight my instinct to stay silent.

At church, I'd see Polk, on the other side of the sanctuary. I admired him for standing in front of strangers and revealing parts of his life that so many people would have kept hidden. When Pastor Strong asked members to go shake hands with someone they didn't know, I walked over to Polk, introduced myself, and told him that I had been at the men's breakfast. I said I'd never been in prison, but I'd had my own troubles, and I considered him courageous for talking about his in front of strangers.

One Sunday, when I wasn't looking forward to the workweek, I felt a strong hand on my shoulder. I turned and saw Polk. He wanted to know how I was doing. I shrugged. He said he'd pray for me.

"Lay down your burden," he told me.

If God puts the right person in your life at the right time, Joshua Polk was meant for me. I wasn't as interested in how he came to faith—I was long past deciding whether I believed— or what he thought of the Bible. What intrigued me was how he dealt with failure, and what role

What intrigued me was how he dealt with failure.

faith had in giving him a sense of hope and not letting a label— *felon*—define him as a man, husband, and father.

He invited me to his home one evening. His wife was busy in the kitchen, and we sat in the living room, where he told me his story. He'd grown up in Portland, the child of a good family, one that went to church, did all the right things, and was respected in the community. But the lure of the streets—mostly easy money—was too attractive, and he moved up from small-time dealing to being a major player.

Polk was one of twenty-seven people—most of them friends—who landed in jail. The bust was big news and was featured in the newspaper and on television stations. People in the neighborhood, his parents' friends, and people he'd gone to school with all knew what had happened.

Reality truly hit in the courtroom when the judge rapped the gavel and handed down the sentence. During the first few weeks in prison, Polk reflected on every poor choice he'd made. What was he going to do next, and how was he going to spend the next twelve years?

"I saw a guy kill himself in prison," he said. "What I went through breaks people. You have to be strong. You can't show weakness. You can't admit fear. I couldn't change where I was, but I vowed that I wouldn't leave prison the same man that I'd been on the street."

I told Polk that made sense, but it was also a stereotype based on what I knew about prisoners, parolees, and ex-cons through stories I'd written over the years. In the joint, everyone seems to reach out to God. About the only person who can quote Bible passages better than a street preacher is an inmate. I once sat across from a serious, hard-core inmate who had been an enforcer for a street gang. His job was collecting debt and protecting turf. But when I was with him, he didn't want to talk about the past, only about Jesus Christ and what he'd studied in the Bible that morning. A year later, he was released; not six months later, he was back in trouble.

The way I saw it, the inmate was cutting a deal with the supreme cop. Faith was an excuse, a way to get a pass on what he'd done.

When I was writing those stories, I had no faith in my life, but even someone like myself could see the superficiality of what they professed to believe. I met a woman, a heavy user of meth, cocaine, and marijuana, who was sent to prison for being the getaway driver in an armed robbery where a clerk was murdered for a few hundred dollars. When I interviewed her in prison, she told me she'd changed her life. God was helping her. As part of my story, I followed her after she got out. The moment she was handed her parole papers, she forgot about God. The Bible was just another book she'd read in prison. She drifted back into drugs and crime. Within two years, she was back in prison. When I checked in with her to see how she was doing and what she'd learned, she told me she was reading the Bible again.

Polk told me he'd met people just like that in prison, caught up in God and Jesus because it was a distraction from prison. For many, it had no more meaning than time in the recreation yard.

"For me it was an evolution," Polk said. "You have to remember that I had fallen away from faith when I was in the drug world. But in prison, faith wasn't about words or me making grand statements. I didn't even tell anyone about it."

He went to the prison library and began looking for books

on self-improvement. None of them touched his soul. It was all words on a page. And they weren't enough. One day he moved to another shelf in the library and stumbled upon a book about faith and spirituality. He read one page. Then another. He kept reading, feeling something stir within him for the first time in years. In that library he made himself a promise, vowing to use faith and God to change his life. He didn't become a prison preacher or announce that he'd been saved. All he did was wake up each morning and try to be a better man than he had been the day before.

"God was pulling on the strings of my heart," he said. "I'd walked away from Him, but He hadn't abandoned me. You cannot come to Jesus unless God draws you to him. I was starting a spiritual evolution where I could once again respect and honor God the way I had when I was a boy."

One day Polk went to the prison chapel. If a man is sick, he goes to the prison infirmary. The chapel, Polk figured, would be the place where he could find the information, the road map he needed to continue his journey. He found Bibles and books about theology, but was drawn to, of all things, a cassette tape of gospel music, the sound track to his childhood and a more innocent time in life. He inserted the tape in a machine and adjusted the volume. The music and lyrics transported him to a better place. He closed his eyes. He wasn't thinking, only feeling, letting the music minister to his heart and soul. And in that chapel, for the first time in years, he wept.

"That wasn't the most powerful and strong thing a man could do in a federal prison," he said. "But I didn't care who saw me. God was doing a miraculous work in my life; He was changing me from the inside out."

I told Polk that his name—Joshua—had meaning to someone I'd met on my faith journey. Marty Guise, the man with the son who had Tourette's syndrome, told me that in his low moments he'd turned to the Bible for strength. In the book of Joshua, he found the phrase "be strong and courageous."

But what happens when we're not strong? What happens when we're weak and afraid?

Guise told me that he studied the Hebrew word for *strong* and came to believe that it did not mean "physically strong." It meant "to fasten ourselves to God." That takes courage because we must surrender control. Prison is a pretty obvious sign of hitting bottom. But all of us hit bottom. Maybe it's not as obvious as being locked up, but in the quiet of our souls, each of us knows the truth.

"God is concerned with your heart," Polk said. "Man looks at outward things and puts on a show because we are concerned how we look to others."

I told Polk I could relate.

"When I made that faith commitment in prison, I was all in," he said. "I was ostracized by some other inmates. Some people are uncomfortable with change, especially when you start talking about faith. For a man it's better to talk about being strong and tough. Faith talk can cause confusion. Sometimes people turn away from you. Some inmates thought I was nuts. Once they realized I was serious about faith, they stopped talking to me.

"Then God brings people into your life," he said. "I met a seventy-one-year-old white guy who became one of my best friends. Faith is what brought us together. We formed a support group in the prison that met every week."

As much as faith made sense in prison, I wanted to know what happened when Polk got out. How did he come back to the community and not feel shamed? How did he deal with people he thought were friends, but who abandoned him, shunned him when all he needed was an encouraging word?

The transition wasn't easy. Some people slipped out of his life—some by his choice and some by theirs. He learned who was a friend and who wasn't. He saw his old world with a clarity shaped by hard times.

"I was a reborn man," he said. "By that, I mean that I had, and still have, a relationship with Jesus Christ. In essence, I took my hand off the steering wheel and trusted God to get me where I was supposed to go."

That act of surrendering—what Guise called courageous—was as hard as anything Polk had ever attempted.

"As men, we want to fix everything and act like we're in control even though we know that isn't true," he said. "A guy will always say he's 'OK' or 'doing great' when that's not always the case. If you ask how things are going, I could tell you fine. But that wouldn't be the truth. Right now, all hell has broken loose. My wife was fired from her job and my son is in trouble."

He paused, letting the words sink in.

"I don't try to understand why or take control," Polk said. "I have to find strength in my relationship with God."

I told Polk what it was like when I went back to work, standing outside the newspaper building and saying a prayer for strength. He leaned forward, reached out, and shook my hand.

Men hide their pain and doubts from each other, he said, and because of that, we approach faith differently than women. Faith is too often seen as a sign of weakness in a man. So they leave praying, reading the Bible, and church to the wife, aunt, or grandmother. Sometimes, he said, men need a slap up against the head, a reminder that they aren't so strong. What happened to me, he told me, was a slap. He knew I liked to box. He asked me what happened when I got hit. I could crumble or I could dig deep and push on. What I

couldn't do was quit the fight. Just like we can't check out of
life when it gets tough.

"Most everything I had in my life was taken away from
me," he said. "I was starting at square one. Outside of a little
money I'd earned in prison, I didn't have much. I was a man
with scars. Much of the world saw me as a failure."

He fell silent.

"All I had," he said, "was my faith and my story."

But that was enough to rebuild a life.

"There's a potential for healing there," he said. "We are
only as sick as our secrets. It's the stuff we hold inside that
kills. Faith and trust in God gives us the confidence to embrace our pain and let God use it for good."

I told him I knew all about keeping secrets.

"Tom, your story is someone else's story," he said. "By telling your story to others, you build a relationship and that
makes it okay for others to tell their stories. God is magnified
when people can see where God has brought you from and
what He has established in you."

He, too, knows the struggle of feeling judged.

"When my wife was fired, she was telling people what had
happened," he said. "I wanted her to shut up. I felt such
shame. I didn't want her telling everyone our business. But she
didn't listen to me. She kept talking. People rallied behind her
and supported her as she went through what had happened.
Power comes from sharing with others. In a sense we're all
ministers."

So what about his daughter and his son? Neither attends
church. His daughter was going to college. His son was in
trouble with the law. Why not make them go to church? I
often wondered, I told him, if I would have been a better father to my kids if I had been an example by going to church.

"God is not in your face," he said. "He does not force us to come to Him. We get to choose. You have to make the choice on your own. Not everyone makes the choice. Is that God's fault, or our fault?

"I saw a guy walking down the street the other day that I grew up with," Polk said. "He was talking to himself. He had some bad drugs, was out of his mind, and didn't recognize me. Without faith, that could have been me. Faith gives me perspective and an appreciation for what I have. In a sense I died and came back.

"I'm not just talking about prison," he said. "I experienced a spiritual death, and my rebirth is symbolized in baptism. You are dipped in the water and the life as you knew it is over, and you are resurrected as a new man.

"Fear is a huge part of the faith journey," he said. "The stuff you are bitter and shameful about can be healing if you let it go. What happens, though, is that you keep all that stuff inside because you believe that if people find out about it, you will be judged. In fact, it's the opposite. At that men's meeting, I was vulnerable. That's what drew you in."

When Polk came out of prison, he debated about moving from Portland, starting over, and never talking about his past.

"The Bible teaches us that when we commit our lives to Christ, old things are passed away and we are a new creation in Christ," he said. "Guilt over our actions is not a place God wants us to be as Christians. Faith is believing that God is serious about that redemption and a new start. The Bible is full of examples of people who've blown it, stories of men who have fallen short, and stories of men who are good but who have made mistakes.

"Think about the mistakes you've made, Tom, and the ones I've made," he said. "It was those mistakes that have the power to make us the people we will become if we use faith and the love of God to transform ourselves. I don't think I could have had the perspective and outlook, the thirst and hunger and appreciation for how my life is now, if I hadn't come so close to losing it."

When we fall, or make a mistake, our instinct—especially with men—is to hide, act like it doesn't matter, or lash out in anger.

"That's standing at the crossroads," he said. "Who hasn't been at the crossroads? You hide in shame, or you step into the light. When you confront your past mistakes and talk about them, you find a peace.

"That takes all the power away from the naysayers who want to use your mistakes to condemn you," he said. "When you share openly and honestly, all the bullets from your enemies fall to the ground.

"In the lowest times of our lives, we are not alone," he said. "God is there. We can be our own worst enemies, depending on how we want to deal with our past and mistakes. What I'm learning through faith is that rather than my mistakes being a hitching post, something I tie myself to, I want my mistakes to be a guidepost on my journey. What faith does is allow us to move forward and become the individual God wants us to be."

His honesty at the men's group, I told him, showed me he was a man I could talk to about my life, problems, and worries. I told him I wanted to be that person for someone else who was struggling.

"The first time I shared my story, I prayed for strength," he said. "I could hardly get through it without shedding a tear. But something miraculous happened. Every time I tell my story, it gets a little easier. That's the healing process. I don't pretend to be intelligent enough to have it all figured out, but there's something to us being vulnerable and transparent.

"We draw strength from the men who are open about their

shortcomings. There's nothing more powerful than hearing a man who is secure enough to stand before others and share how they dropped the ball.

"If we're honest with each other, who hasn't made a mistake?" he said. "How can you be forty or fifty and not have some secrets that are a little embarrassing? God works through us to allow us to step out of ourselves. That's the power of people sharing their stories.

"The perfect man does not exist," he said. "The guy pretending to be perfect is a fraud. If his life was to pop up on the video monitor in the front of the church, I guarantee you, he'd get up and run out of the building."

It was getting late, and Polk had to be up early for work. He walked me to the door. Instead of shaking my hand, he hugged me.

"For some of us," he said, "our lives and stories are out there already."

Joshua Polk climbed the steps at the hotel and walked down the hallway to the room where his son said he could find him. He saw the door ajar and stepped inside. Polk, always aware of his surroundings, noticed seedy characters. His son emerged from a back room and pointed toward him.

"This is my father," his son told the room. "We need to talk."

The men joined the others hanging on the balcony. Polk and his son sat on chairs. As Polk listened to his son speak about this latest round of trouble, he knew the cops would be involved.

A cop attended Life Change Center. On Sunday Polk would seek her out, admit his son was in trouble. He would ask her advice and counsel, and in doing so admit that not all was perfect in his life. The man with a rap sheet, the man who came to church each Sunday, had a son who could end up going to jail.

Polk wrapped his arms around his son, held him close, and prayed out loud, not caring if the gangbangers heard him: "God, place angels around this boy so he is not hurt. God, capture his heart again."

Polk told his son he loved him. He kissed him on the check. He left the room, walked down the stairs and across the parking lot. He opened his car door, turned the ignition, and put the car in drive.

He took a final look at the room.

He prayed again.

"God, my son knows me. He knows what I have done. Let him bear witness to the transformative power of Jesus Christ in his father's life. Please, God, let my son see how his father lives now."

He hit the gas, the headlights cutting through the night and leading him back home.

"Are you tired? Worn out? Burned out on religion?
Come to me. Get away with me and you'll recover your life.
I'll show you how to take a real rest.
Walk with me and work with me—watch how I do it.
Learn the unforced rhythms of grace.
I won't lay anything heavy or ill-fitting on you.
Keep company with me
and you'll learn to live freely and lightly."

—Matthew 11:28–30

"It's Jesus speaking words of guidance.
Tom, lay down your weariness and worry.
Join Jesus in daily living and enjoy the deepening process
of experiencing Christ's love, gentleness, and humility.
Be aware of gratitude for the gift in all experiences
and for the mentors who are put alongside you.
Be in balance of solitude with God
and activity for good, in large and small.
Let yourself be loved by Jesus
and give that love to others around you."

—*Gayle Heuser*

CHAPTER 18

Faith Counselor

After years of talking, contemplating, and meeting people of faith, I wanted to make sense of where I had been and where I was going. At times, I felt as if I'd returned from a long vacation with thousands of photographs, each one marking a moment that had been important but now lacked meaning.

The feeling reminded me of what it was like after spending months immersed in someone's life for one of my long-form narrative pieces. A good editor would listen while I talked out the story. In the conversation I knew what I needed in terms of structure and scene to guide the reader.

This stop on my journey, I now knew, is where people quit going to church or drift away from faith. The problem isn't boredom or disbelief. It's lack of direction. The initial excitement had worn off, and what remains are new and different questions.

During this fallow period, I heard about someone who was a spiritual director. A man I knew—a man of great faith—went to this woman on a regular basis and described her as someone who served as a kind of faith counselor who serves as a guide for those on the journey.

I got her name, called her, and told her I'd never heard of

a spiritual counselor. I asked if it was one of those new-age things that pops up from time to time.

Gayle Heuser told me the ministry of spiritual direction has a long and honored place in Christian history. In the New Testament she said a "discerning, companioning relationship" was shown in Jesus and his disciples.

That spiritual mentoring continued in the early church, from apostles and desert mothers and fathers to bishops. John Cassian, a monk who lived from 360 to 435, she told me, was a spiritual director who introduced an intentional process of mentoring into monasteries. In the 1200s, the Dominican order of itinerant friars emphasized the regular care of souls for spiritual discernment and wholeness. In time, the practice of spiritual direction spread beyond the monastery.

Heuser told me she grew up in a Lutheran home and her passion was music. After college she sang professionally for fifteen years. At age thirty she came to know Jesus—quite powerfully, she emphasized—when a friend suggested she explore the Bible. She'd previously read it, but not with any depth.

"One evening, feeling very much alone in the world and on another continent, I was reading Matthew 11:28–30 and I 'heard' Jesus speak those words to me," she said. "The words seemed to come right off the page and into my awareness from a presence in my room who I knew was Christ. To this day I have tears when I consider it.

"The gift of the awareness that Christ is present with me continues," she said. "After that initial experience, different things occurred similarly perhaps to when you talk about going to your church. You said you felt the Spirit speaking to your heart as well as to your mind. That connection, that integration between heart and mind, is what has occurred over time."

Since that encounter with Christ, Heuser became aware of being drawn deeper into more integration of her faith. She trained to be a spiritual director and became more aware of the journey God has for her. She said it brings her joy to know that she is a small part of something much greater that is happening here and now.

People come to a spiritual director who listens and remains attentive to what the spirit might be doing in that person's life. She described herself as something like a midwife. The spirit does the work of healing and drawing the person into a deeper love relationship with God.

"Maybe you got a taste of something like that when you went to that church and you heard something was said that was 'just for you,'" she told me. "God knows you and your fears and heart and gave you something that penetrated. That's a sign that you're being drawn into this deeper relationship."

When I was in Southern California, I called and set up a session with her, believing that she could help with my faith malaise.

I'd asked my wife if she wanted to go to church with me, and during the service I paid as much attention to her reaction as to what was being said.

A church and, by extension, faith are so personal that I wanted my wife to appreciate it the way I did. As I said earlier, she grew up in a Lutheran church, sang all the hymns, and knew all the liturgy. After high school she quit going, returning to her church only for our wedding, a few social events, and her father's funeral.

As we were driving home from what she now called my church, I asked her what she thought. She said she enjoyed some parts, but others did nothing for her. I tried to convince her that she was wrong. By the time we arrived home, I realized I was trying to sell her on this place and how I saw faith instead of letting her experience it and get what she wanted, or didn't want, out of it.

I continued to go to church by myself and felt a freedom in doing it just for me. When I arrived home, I'd change out of my Sunday clothes and talk with my wife, telling her how I was going to use what I'd learned during my upcoming week.

At one point I asked her what she thought of this journey of mine and why I'd embarked on it. Had I changed? I was too close to the subject, obviously, and needed the perspective of someone who knew me well.

She sent me this e-mail:

It's interesting to me that, as a journalist, you gravitated to the human interest stories with people who had such sadness, loss, and unfairness in their lives. Often you came away from writing these stories noticing that those you wrote about had found a way to cope through some kind of faith or belief.

Why were you the one to write these stories? How is it that time and again people who read your work would comment on how your writing made them feel strong emotions? If you believe you have a purpose in life, and that is to be a great storyteller, then it is like a kind of mission you seem to be on.

I think you feel that you are supposed to write and give a voice to people. It would follow, then, that if you have the gift to write, who are you grateful to for that gift? The seed of faith is when you want to show gratitude for all that has been given to you.

The big change happened for you when you began to realize that you could feel helpless, alone, even suffering with your own challenges in life. There wasn't anyone interviewing you or offering you insight to feelings of aloneness, loss, disappointment, disillusionment. You were looking within yourself for answers.

You were more than just a writer, but you were feeling your own humanity and hiding behind your own self-doubts. You wanted to find what it was that others rely on during times of trial and tribulation, a sense of something, maybe someone bigger than you.

What I have noticed about this journey you are on is that you haven't fallen to your knees with a desperate acceptance of God and Jesus. You have quietly seen in others something you wanted for yourself.

Faith is not the absence of doubt, but it is the choice to allow faith to trump doubt or to suspend disbelief in favor of a peace within. You don't need to preach or tally up all you witness to, but it is a quiet walk down an unknown path that shows your life's calling, purpose, and gratitude to something or someone you cannot prove to anyone else, but you would hope that others may see that you stopped to notice and show reverence to.

Gayle Heuser answered the door to her home on the first knock and led me into her living room. I sat in a chair; she, on a sofa. She explained that most of the people she sees have an ongoing relationship with her, much the way someone might have with a therapist.

"The spirit directs the questions," she told me. "Something happens, and I'm there to provide a place of hospitality. The spirit whispers something, a truth to you. Your questions would evolve into answers about your faith.

"I sense you are struggling with faith," she said. "The people who come here want to know God's love more deeply. What you need is a little bit of faith. God does the rest."

She asked me to close my eyes. She read a prayer and asked me to think about what words touched me, and to feel the spirit within me. The spirit within me? It brought back memories of when I was in college and found myself onstage when a visiting hypnotist asked for volunteers. He then "hypnotized" us, instructing us to lift our arms, act like we were swimming, and touching a hot stove. I was never under a spell, but played along for the fun of it.

But as Heuser prayed, I did feel something in me. Certain words made me think about my life, my faith journey, and the people I'd met along the way. It was as if I were watching a slide show: Annette, Jacqui, Pastor Red, and the gravesite where little Jonah Van Arnam was buried.

We started to talk. She often answered my question with a question. When I asked if we need faith, and wondered what we got out of it, she bounced it back to me: What do you believe in? Who do you believe in?

I told her I believed in God and Jesus. But I've also discovered the words *God, Jesus,* and even *Christian* can be used by others to label me. I feel the presence of a God who gives meaning to my life. I'm no longer looking for a definite answer. My search for proof of faith has ended. But I still struggle, at times, when I don't get what I want out of being faithful. When I hear about tragedies happening to good people or when I run into tough times, I feel like God has let me down.

I know that doesn't make sense. One of my faith teachers told me that attitude turns me back into myself. What has become clear is that I see faith and God played out in the lives of people I write about.

"It sounds like you are coming to know your God in your own unique way," she said. "I guess that would be a really fitting description for many of us. How stage-by-stage and season-by-season, we may come to know more of God—and therefore, more of ourselves.

"Because each person is a unique creature—right down to his or her own fingerprint—it follows that everyone has a different experience of God," she told me. "Each of us has been given a life like that of no one else, and we each have the opportunity during our short span of days to let God walk with us where no one else can go.

"This is very much a relational process, isn't it?" she asked me. "It's one of trust and learning to trust. When you first started talking, the word that jumped out to me was *vulnerable*. You were noticing that you were drawn to the Spirit in this church.

"That is a gift," she said. "The Spirit drawing you is a precious gift that many aren't aware of. You are open to it, and it sounds like your vulnerability has caused you to really crave more of knowing who this God is and who you are in light of that. It is a very gentle and mysterious process of growth to say I believe."

Heuser told me that faith is a gift we can't create for ourselves. The gift is a realization that God's love draws us to Him.

"We're not the ones growing ourselves," she said. "The Spirit is at work in us and draws us to trust more deeply, to grow and know incrementally, the love of God that is so abundant in everything around us.

"Even as I learn the lessons of trust," she said, "there are so many layers of myself that still ask, 'Can I really trust you?' What helps me are spiritual disciplines like prayer, solitude, and spiritual direction that can help me to make trusting choices, however small they might be, every day."

Is it better to grow in faith incrementally, the way I have? Why don't we grow all at once and be done with it?

"Yes, why indeed?" she asked. "Why do we grow as children at certain rates? Maybe that question could be rephrased in a different way. What is it like for you when you live with the fact that growth means one step forward and two steps backward? And then two steps forward and one back?"

I told her it was frustrating, but because of other interests in my life, I could understand the process. When a person starts studying karate, he's given a white belt—the sign of a rank novice. Over the years, he progresses through a series of other colored belts—yellow, orange, blue, purple, brown, and then black. My sensei in New York City told me that people think the black belt is the final destination. Over the decades, though, the black starts to fade. In time, it is nearly white. And the circle is completed.

I'd been reading Proverbs, but even when I read a passage I had read numerous times, I always found it meant something different to me. I was wiser than I'd once been, but still a novice.

"That is the heart of living the mystery of faith," she said. "These are the types of mysterious realities and paradoxes that people, like you and me and the readers, are so hungry to fathom. We learn to live in the paradox of yes I am growing, but it may not look like what I think it should look like.

"Paradox runs throughout the Scripture," she said. "Like one must 'lose' his or her life in order to gain it, one must let go of all obvious treasure to gain the real treasure, embracing both God's sovereignty and free will, and the idea of faith and works."

I asked why I was still sometimes reluctant to fully embrace faith outside of church. I felt like it defined me because it allowed other people to determine what faith meant to them and then ascribe those qualities to me.

"That's difficult for you, huh?" she said. "We are all going to be labeled by each other. It's part of our own insecurity with each other. When someone takes that first step in the journey of faith, there's a newness and excitement that feels so 'right.' The new believer desires everyone else to experience that and to feel the same way—to mirror back that feeling, consequently the tracts and the enthusiasm that can be off-putting.

"But there are many stages to the development of faith," she said. "And at times we may be given a glimpse into the reality of a saying attributed to St. Francis of Assisi: 'Preach the Gospel at all times; if necessary, use words.' To me it implies the paradox that my actions have power just as the words I use have power."

In the same way that Pastor Mark Strong had spoken about "doing good," Heuser said that caring for the disenfranchised in society, living one's life moment-by-moment from a center of love, compassion, and peace, and being generous and kind in small and large things are the ways we preach the Gospel, whether in our homes or out in society.

As the journey of faith continues and we mature, she said, we become aware of areas for which we are responsible in new ways. Perhaps it is telling the truth with a new level of courage or realizing that we need to give away more and keep less.

"As a spiritual director, I am privileged to be with people— present to those who are very different than I am and in different stages of life and faith," she said. "I receive the grace I need to be with them and to let them be who they are. It takes time for that to develop. Our time is different than God's time."

Even two weeks ago, I told her, my faith felt different when I was at church. It wasn't as powerful or alluring—even as intoxicating—as it had been years earlier.

"It sounds like what you are expressing is an important part of the faith journey," she said. "Some would say that the Spirit is always drawing us into ever-deepening relationship.

As you respond to that 'ever-deepening' growth, it follows that some of the experiences you enjoyed in the past might not satisfy you now.

"I believe we cannot draw ourselves to that which is larger than we are," she said. "To beauty, wonder, awe, rest, peace. God's Spirit draws me insofar as I am available, present, and receptive. These are attitudes I deeply value and practice.

"Some signs of being drawn are refreshment rather than anxiety," she said. "Being okay with uncertainty, mystery, and gentle curiosity. Think of when something in nature comes as a surprise into your awareness with its appearance of beauty or wonder. A close-up with a hummingbird, for instance. Another paradoxical refreshment: feeling remorse for the wrong I've done."

She told me that as her connection with God grows deeper, some of the things that brought her joy when she was thirty-five no longer hold the same meaning.

"But something else does," she said. "We go through these phases of dryness where the same type of thing does not work. We are growing in our faith."

Several people I'd met during the past few years told me that faith is a gift. Heuser told me it was a blessing that I felt stirrings when I went to Life Change Christian Center on a routine assignment.

"Faith is a free gift to all people," she said. "God loves and desires good for all people. I believe each person has a choice about how to respond. We see people of great faith coming from very poor and difficult backgrounds. And we see great faith that has come out of backgrounds that don't look difficult to our eyes. It's an individual response to the invitation."

I asked if she thought all people were presented with that gift. Why did some people answer faith's call while others claimed to have never heard it?

"What do you think?" she asked. "We all see some gifts and reject others. Sometimes it takes a while for us to see things as 'gifts.' But God is very patient with us. It's a relational process. God is always beckoning us. Come closer, come home, there is grace here for you. Set everything down, come and rest."

Bottom line, then, what do we get by being faithful? What's your best sales pitch for someone wavering?

"A very good spiritual-direction question," she said. "What happened when you decided to avail yourself to the gift of God's love at that church? What did you get out of it?"

I'd say a sense of peace, a sense that I am not in control, and a sense of vulnerability. Also an awareness of my own flaws. I'm aware of parts of myself that I'd like to change.

"Beautifully said," she smiled. "You encapsulated so wonderfully the mystery of faith. There's a sense of peace despite the fact that there's a letting go. That's a spiritual truth. Letting go is a daily response to God.

"And yet you express a sense of peace, which I imagine has something to do with feeling compassion and a greater love for yourself and others," she said. "There is hope mingled in there, too, a reason for living. And meaning. Meaning is essential for wholeness.

"At the same time there's humility in saying you are able to look at yourself and know that you are not able to do this on your own," she said. "You are not sufficient, and you are in need of something and someone much bigger than you are. Isn't that great? What a gorgeous paradox that is."

"You are not sufficient, and you are in need of something and someone much bigger than you are. Isn't that great?"

During the past few years, I'd heard so often about what

we get out of a relationship with God, but what does God get?

"Well, while I don't know what God gets out of it," she said, "I do know that God values connection, forgiveness, creativity, beauty, wonder, possibility, justice, and love, to name just a few qualities. Reading the Bible is one of the essential ways to respond to the connection, because it's a living text."

I told her that I still had a difficult time reading the Bible. At church, the pastor would build a sermon around a few phrases, which I found easier to grasp than sitting down each night and reading.

She suggested I read just a few words of scripture and see what struck me. Let the words do the work within me, going so far as to ask God to speak to me through the words. Studying the scripture takes many forms—all appropriate, depending on where the reader is on the journey.

"In Psalm 46 there's a beautiful word cluster: *Be still and know I am God*," she said. "By the way, some would interpret the Hebrew text for 'be still' as 'lay it down.' You could read that and sit with it. Ask God if there is something God wants to say to you through those words. Meditate. Let those words roll through your heart and mind.

"Some people start at the beginning, and by the time they get to Leviticus, they run into rules about dietary restrictions and think they will never get through the Bible," she said. "Yes, read the whole Bible, but get to know different books that will speak to you for different seasons and places where you are. Enjoy the various sections of scripture—the psalms, the Prophets, the Gospels, and the letters.

"Reading the Bible is like going to a big art museum and realizing that you're not going to be able to see every painting," she said. "But maybe one or three pieces that afternoon just jump out at you. They resonate with you. You ponder those paintings, and next time you go there, you might see different ones, but you start knowing where to go."

Heuser told me that when she needs hope and inspiration, she turns to Isaiah and reads key verses that have become what she calls friends of hers. Through them, she believes, God speaks to her.

"At times in my life when I wonder why something is happening, I go to this truth—God is always on the move making something into good," she said. "He has spoken to me many times through Isaiah, especially about restoring and reconciling."

Part of me is impatient with the pace of the faith journey. Maybe going to the ocean, looking at the waves, and feeling peace is enough.

"Tom, you're not alone," she said. "Many of us wonder about these things. If you are especially drawn to the scripture, read and ask God to show you what you are to be aware of. Notice where you are drawn. What might God want to give you?"

I told her I didn't know. Some Sundays I'd be in church and my mind would wander. Other times, even a rerun of an old *Law and Order* was more compelling than God, the Bible, and faith. At least at the end of the show there's a moment when everything is wrapped up.

"I think that what you are describing is one reason that, in a life of faith, there come times of dryness," she said. "God's love for us is a powerful call. Our loving response is learning to listen and to take right action. One way to open to God's love is through centering prayer, or soaking prayer.

"But this is a gift to which you respond with gratitude and then gradually God grows you in the ability to be more centered and more aware of this love around you," she said. "Just as gentle as a plant growing."

Are faith journeys easy to start and then get harder? Or are they hard to start and then they get easier?

"I think it's different for each person," she said. "Do you have kids? You remember what that was like going through growth periods? Children grow in different ways at different times."

Does God get disappointed in us on our journey? Does He say come on and hurry up?

"Do you feel impatient with yourself at times?"

I'm not sure.

"Do you feel God has you on a timetable?" she asked. "The Scriptures say that Jesus Christ stands at the door and knocks. He is always waiting for us to come to the door, but will always leave it up to us to respond. He is infinite goodness and loves each human so perfectly—respects each person's free will so completely—that He will never force himself upon us. But then, he has all the time in the world."

Are there times you feel God's absence?

"I am no different than anyone else," she said. "Many changes happen during the course of our lives. For instance, I'm discovering what I've read about: that the first half of life is one of strengthening our egos, of being generative and productive and 'moving upward.'

"The second part of life is one of acceptance and letting go—of embracing the things that are most real and seem to have eternal meaning," she said. "It makes sense that as our self and our sense of morality and ethical perspective change, that we see God and ourselves differently.

"This includes our perception of our personal image of God," she said. "A perceived feeling of absence may be an indication that some transformation is happening within us, and that we cannot rely on the old 'maps' anymore. That's not a bad thing, but it can feel disorienting at the time.

"What helps me personally is the Holy Spirit, friendship with Jesus and with people whom God has put in my sphere," she said. "And that's what is available to every person. What did you hear me say there?"

The road to faith is so foggy. What does it mean? When does it end? How do I, or any of us, know how we are making progress?

"It is uncharted territory because it's uniquely your journey," she said. "However, here's where you could 'make friends' with the scripture—and more importantly, with the God of the text: Hebrews 11 says that faith is confidence in what we hope for and assurance about what we do not see.

"Perhaps as you journey on, you will receive some surprising assurances," she said. "Maybe you will see some fruit of the Spirit blooming in yourself like love, joy, peace, patience, kindness, goodness, gentleness, faithfulness, self-control."

Where should I go?

"I can hear from your enthusiasm and curiosity that God is at work," she said. "You are being drawn and you are right where you need to be. Trust that, be attentive. Enjoy gratitude for the gift in all experiences and for the mentors that are put alongside you. Let yourself be loved by Jesus and give that love to others around you."

She had one final thought.

"The image of God is reflected in aspects of you," she said. "Don't try to be anything but you."

Back in Portland, I once again thought of Annette Steele. What would she tell me to do? I reached for my Bible—the one whose pages are crinkled because I've actually used it—and closed my eyes, just the way she did more than fifty years ago when she was looking for an answer. I flipped the pages,

stopped, ran my fingers down one page, and stopped again, on
Isaiah 30:8–11:

> So, go now and write all this down. Put it in a book
> So that the record will be there to instruct the coming
>   generations,
> Because this is a rebel generation, a people who lie,
> A people unwilling to listen to anything God tells them.
> They tell their spiritual leaders, "Don't bother us with
>   irrelevancies."
> They tell their preachers, "Don't waste our time on
>   impracticalities.
> Tell us what makes us feel better. Don't bore us with
>   obsolete religion.
> That stuff means nothing to us, Quit hounding us with
>   The Holy of Israel."

Just make sure you stay alert.
Keep close watch over yourselves.
Don't forget anything of what you've seen.
Don't let your heart wander off.
Stay vigilant as long as you live.
Teach what you've seen and heard
to your children and grandchildren.

—Deuteronomy 4:9

"I'm little more than a rank novice
when it comes to the Bible.
My method is still to flip through the pages,
land on something,
read the passage, and try to find the meaning
and relevance for my life.
This passage struck me and reminded me
of my own mortality.
In the years to come, I hope that my children remember
not what I did for a living, but how I lived."

—Tom Hallman, Jr.

CHAPTER 19

Completing the Circle

One Father's Day, I told my two daughters that I didn't want any gifts. All I wanted was for them to go to church with me. I hoped it would be a better experience for them than it had been for me when my mother asked me to go with her, so many decades ago, on Mother's Day.

I wasn't sure what I wanted them to get out of the experience. I wasn't trying to recruit them or make them feel guilty.

Surprisingly, I didn't have to do any arm-twisting. Over the years, I'd shared stories about who I met on my faith journey. They told me that I'd taught them that faith could relate to their lives.

If so, then my journey had been worthwhile.

Pastor Mark Strong's sermon that Sunday was about isolation and loneliness. He spoke about the Facebook generation and how insidious and damaging it was to the soul and spirit it was to believe that true friends are but a click away on a computer screen.

They agreed.

As much as I thought I was teaching my daughters about faith, it was my oldest daughter who taught me a lesson that Sunday. When the service ended, I introduced my children to some of the members.

We were about to leave church when Joshua Polk jogged over to me. He shook my hand and told me my daughters—Rachael and Hanna—were beautiful.

I asked how his son was doing.

He shook his head. Not well.

What about his daughter?

"Tom," he said, "I'm worried. You know how much I want her to have an education. She's been in college, but now she tells me she wants to quit. I just don't know what to do. She doesn't realize how it will impact her life."

I offered a few words of advice, but they fell flat.

But then I watched faith up close and in action.

"Don't worry," Rachael told Polk. "I took time off from college. She can go back. I bet she goes back."

There, in front of me, was faith's circle.

It was Polk who had once told me to lay my burden down. He helped me find my way back again by sharing his story. And here now, it was a stranger—my daughter—who said the words that he needed to hear.

Faith's mystery, power, love, and ability to heal: all were on display in a small section of a church long after services had ended.

I knew more now than I had when I stepped into this church seven years ago, a reporter just doing his job.

But as a man, I had so much more to learn.

"Josh," I said, "I'll see you next Sunday."

ACKNOWLEDGMENTS

A storyteller is nothing without a story. I am grateful for all who let me into their lives to talk about faith and what it means to them. All of you have given me the best gift possible: your hearts and souls.

My agent, Noah Lukeman, saw the beginnings of this book when we were talking about our lives during a breakfast in New York City. He championed it at every step. He is a good man and a good friend.

I could not have worked with a better editor than Philis Boultinghouse, a senior editor at Howard Books. She knew when to push me and also when to support me. Her instincts and ability serve as a reminder that every writer needs a talented editor as a partner.

Jessica Wong, an associate editor, oversaw so many critical details of this project.

Andrea Peabbles, copy editor, read my story with care and precision.

Davina Mock-Maniscalco, interior designer, made these pages inviting to readers.

Bruce Gore, cover designer, brilliantly captured the essence of this book.